Gravitas is the playbook for spiritually and emotionally of influence.

MIKE MATZINGER, PhD, president of Burlington Chemical Co.

In *Gravitas*, Jerome has bridged the gap between spiritual leadership and business leadership. Combining ancient principles with business practices gives confidence on Monday morning to marry the two realities.

BOBB BIEHL, presidential mentor at Masterplanning Group

Marketplace leaders often feel that leadership success and Christlikeness pull in opposite directions. But what if leadership is the perfect setting for Christlikeness? It can be, and this book illuminates a compelling path for anyone who wants to grow deep to lead large.

CHAD HALL, MCC, director of coaching at Western Seminary

In *Gravitas*, Jerome Daley outlines the process and practices that give a leader true weight. A must-read for anyone ready to deepen their roots and extend their reach.

ANGIE WARD, PhD, leadership author and teacher

Stirring yet practical, drawing on ancient yet relevant principles and practices that are transformative.

FIL ANDERSON, author of *Running on Empty*

With beautifully constructed prose, a passion for leaders to become their best selves, and deeply rooted spirituality, Jerome Daley has created a guidebook that invites engagement with age-old spiritual practices, resulting in real character in the real world.

TINA STOLTZFUS HORST, founder of Coaching Mission International

I wish I had read this book forty years ago!

ED GORE, president and executive director of Fairhaven Ministries

At the beginning of every major spiritual shift in history, God invites men and women into the desert to develop what Jerome Daley refers to as *gravitas*—a spiritual authority gained mostly by enduring loss in God's presence. If you're ready to abandon the endless frenzy of ministry expansion and willing to embrace the quiet rootedness of spiritual substance, *Gravitas* will lead you there.

STEVE WIENS, author of *Shining like the Sun*, *Beginnings*, and *Whole*

This in-depth, captivating book looks into the profoundness of making a mark in the world with the strength of God-sized leadership and authority—the kind of leadership that stems from concentrated time in the presence of God, enabling you to lead with the virtues and lens of Christ.

MARY VERSTRAETE, PCC, leadership coach and consultant

A warmly insightful invitation and guide for living and leading in the real world from a place rooted in true desire, faith, and purpose.

CLIF VAN PUTTEN, MD, anesthesiologist, and DESRIE VAN PUTTEN, branch sales manager at Guarantee Real Estate

A profound and highly practical read. A call to become a leader of weight and depth. *Gravitas* is a game changer.

STEVE KELLER, lead pastor at Cornerstone Community Church, Greeley, CO

With refreshingly clear insight and rare vulnerability, Jerome Daley calls us to a place of spiritual centering for the fruitful and flourishing life that we leaders long for.

STEVE HASE, chair of the Greater Charlotte C12 Group

Surprisingly fresh, modern, and entirely impactful in today's workplace.

JEFFREY BRAMS, ESQ., GC and VP, science and international, at Garden of Life

Well written and challenging in the best of ways, this book is invitation more than admonition; and therein lies its beauty and power.

JEFF HARRIS, president of Jeff Harris and Associates

Succeeds beautifully in helping business leaders create an environment of transformation that our broken world needs so desperately.

DAVID HUGHES, ambassador at the Transforming Center

This book will yield a life of spiritual authority with the ability to swim in an enticing way against the nonstop, depleting world we are living in.

ROY KING, adjunct professor of ministry studies at Columbia International University

This is a valuable and practical guide for deep spiritual-character formation. Daley builds on ancient Christian disciplines to provide insights and inspiration to anyone in Christian leadership who wants to heal and strengthen their soul.

ROBERT A. FRYLING, author of The Leadership Ellipse

The Monastic

Rhythms of

Healthy

Leadership

GRAVITAS

JEROME DALEY

A NavPress resource published in alliance
with Tyndale House Publishers

NavPress is the publishing ministry of The Navigators, an international Christian organization and leader in personal spiritual development. NavPress is committed to helping people grow spiritually and enjoy lives of meaning and hope through personal and group resources that are biblically rooted, culturally relevant, and highly practical.

For more information, visit www.NavPress.com.

Blessed is the one . . .

. . . whose delight is in the law of the Lord,

and who meditates on his law day and night.

That person is like a tree planted by streams of water,

which yields its fruit in season

and whose leaf does not wither—

whatever they do prospers.

PSALM 1:1-3

Contents

Introduction

*What gentler encouragement could we have, my dear brothers
and sisters, than that word from the Lord calling us to himself
in such a way! We can see with what loving concern the
Lord points out to us the path of life.*

RULE OF ST. BENEDICT, prologue

WHO DO YOU KNOW who carries substance as a leader? Not extra-ordinary talent or compelling charisma or impressive expertise, just substance. Weight of character. An unusual presence.

We might call it spiritual gravitas. Such men and women rarely seek the spotlight or dominate the room, but when they speak, you sense that their words rise from a deep core. Intuitively, you know they carry a tensile strength forged in the heat of both victories and defeats. They have paid the price for the truths that now flow from their mouths, words that in turn evoke depths of trust and confidence. You feel drawn to them and secure in their presence, quietly inspired by something that's hard to name.

Other leaders take up an impressive amount of space in a crowd. A commanding voice. Unshakable confidence. Some type of magnetic personality. All eyes turn when they rise . . . and they rise often. You feel drawn to them as well, maybe even electrified by force of personality. But at the end of the day, you're not sure how far you could trust them, not certain you would put your life on the line for them.

Years ago, I attended a small conference. The speaker had a modest following and a few books, but he was only really known within a fairly tight circle. Yet there was something I felt instantly. *Gravitas. Spiritual authority.* I was captivated, and I listened to him for hours without losing interest. Even more, I felt like something deep and true was being mysteriously established in me as he spoke.

The word *gravitas* might evoke images of somber faces and dreary tones, maybe even an intimidating aura, but none of that was true of this speaker. With an easy smile, he spoke softly in slow, thoughtful sentences with very little drama of presentation. It was not exactly a TED Talk, yet I sat rapt with attention, content to let his words wash over me and seep inside.

I think that's the thing about gravitas: It begets more gravitas. I have sometimes imagined myself becoming a dashing, charismatic speaker who could stir crowds and be much in demand. And while there's nothing wrong with that, this guy made me want something different. I found myself wanting to speak from that same deep place, to carry a more grounded substance of being. This man will never know that he set my life course on a new trajectory.

Got Weight?

Gravitas is a Latin word that mirrors our English word *gravity,* anchored in the idea of weight. "Dignity, presence, influence"— these descriptors attempt to capture the effect that such a quality of character has on others.[1] In the social stampede for overt power, there is little demand for gravitas. But when you feel this subtle force in someone, you know instinctively that they are anchored to the earth, immune to the winds of fad and fashion. They don't usually soar in popularity or plunge in ignominy. They are here today and here tomorrow, steadily elevating those around them with kindness and wisdom.

Over the past decade, I have coached many leaders, from starry-eyed entrepreneurs to buttoned-down corporate types, from savvy business owners to burned-out pastors, and all sorts in-between. Each juggles talent and passion; each navigates setbacks and celebrates wins. Coaching is a great job, and I love watching people become the best version of themselves.

Here's the thing: Almost no one hires me for character formation or spiritual growth. People hire me to achieve something that has dollars attached to it: starting a company, writing a book, training a work group, or coaching a key performer. All of these are good things, and I find joy in such meaningful work. *But there is always a bigger story available behind that desire.* Achieving an organizational goal or completing a project is the canvas on which the deeper work of formation is being crafted. And it is the soul more than the project that will endure—which brings us to the heart of the matter.

A Marketplace in Upheaval

Leadership development is a billion-dollar industry. New skills, new techniques, new lingo, new assessments, new gurus, and new books swing in and out of our attention every quarter like revolving ads on a website. There are a lot of smart people showing us how to do more, do it better, and do it faster than ever before. And in many ways, we have benefited from their strategic thinking and best practices. Time management, organizational theory, and marketplace scrutiny have made most of us better at what we do.

The axiom goes, "Work smarter, not harder," but for every leader I know who is absorbing all the "smarts" coming at us so furiously, I see a leader who is indeed working harder. The British philosopher Bertrand Russell speculated in 1932 that if we could merely improve our management expertise in society, the average person need only work four hours a day.[2] About the same time, the economist John Maynard Keynes predicted that by the year 2030, a fifteen-hour workweek would be standard fare.[3] Despite those rosy images, a recent Gallup poll placed the current average workweek at forty-seven hours,[4] and most leaders I know would scoff at such a low number.

How does such a busy world allow for so lofty a concept as gravitas? Seriously, who has the time?

But lack of time for gravitas is killing us.

Leaders are burning out and flaming out at an epic rate. The opposite of gravitas surrounds us and blares from every media channel. Moral failures, abuses of power, and ruthless self-promotion are the more obvious symptoms of our anemic national character. In both ministry and the marketplace, we have succumbed to expediency at the cost of integrity. Where is the rootedness? Where is the humility?

We discuss the public falls with dismay and grieve the more private, personal falls. And mostly, we ignore the quieter alternative to burnout and flameout: numbing out. How many leaders have exchanged their passion for disillusionment and slid softly into autopilot?

We must draw the connection between symptoms and the root cause. *The cause is a lack of roots.* Truly, our culture channels a storm that is uprooting many.

Consider a client of mine. Vince is the president of a small telecom company that, at $25 million in gross profits, is modest within its industry. His company was put on the map by selling and installing pay phones. *When is the last time you saw one of those?* Material things, even the best and smartest, eventually decay. The only thing that kept Vince's company from following their phones into extinction was a prudent shift into an entirely different part of the telecom market, where they are now thriving. They survived a potentially catastrophic market storm.

Storms serve a purpose: They expose dangerously weak foundations and invite new construction to our internal worlds. The greater the external pressure on our lives and leadership, the more God whispers to us in those rare still moments. *Step off the gerbil wheel. You were made for more than turning the economic flywheel of industry. You were made for me! And only in me will you be useful in the workplace.* Can you hear that whisper echo in the subterranean cavities of your soul? That divine invitation hangs in the air, directed to you personally.

Helping Write God's Story

Whether leading in ministry or the marketplace, the men and women I know want to do more than turn a profit and grow an empire; they want to do good in the world. They want to write a redemptive, God-sized story in their spheres. They want their employees to thrive as individuals as well as contribute to the mission. They want the love of God to extend across the planet in ways that ease pain and establish peace. They want the earth to no longer groan under the weight of poverty and pollution and violence. And while they—and all of us—can't do everything, we know in a profound way that we can indeed do something.

Another client owns a successful professional business: Janet Ward and fortyish employees bring in about $5 million a year. Commendable, but not necessarily remarkable. But here's what *is* remarkable: *They give away 10 percent of their revenue!* That's right, they tithe on the gross, putting half a million dollars every year into about fifty nonprofits across the planet that are making life better for tens of thousands.[5] That is spiritual influence. That is something we don't have enough of in today's marketplace.

Spiritual substance. Depth. Weight. Spiritual gravitas. Where could we possibly turn to find a supply of such intangibles? What ancient cache could we open to obtain a spiritual rootedness that can withstand cultural storms and change the world for good in modern times?

A Wealth of Gravitas

What if there was a whole culture of spiritual substance, carefully cultivated over generations, with intentional practices and dedicated focus on the inner life? A leadership community that was all about going deep, not wide? What if there were cloisters of men and women who had anchored themselves in the life of God so that they could speak the words of God with quiet power?

Actually, this is part of our heritage. In Ireland, they were called Celts; in Russia, they were called *poustinikki*; in Egypt, they were called desert fathers and mothers. But the most common and inclusive word for these men and women of spiritual gravitas is *monks*.

The particulars of their lives, the qualifications of their communities, and the emphasis of their spiritual activities were as varied as their times and places dictated. And our own modern world calls for its own applications that relate directly to the needs of our time and place. The lifestyle of the monastery cultivated the very spiritual depth we feel such a dearth of today. *We can no longer meet the complexity of today's leadership challenges from the superficiality and shallowness of today's leadership culture.* We must reach back to a simpler time for deeper resources in order to become "monks in the marketplace."

My Own Gravitas Failures

Let me get personal for a moment. When I speak of leading from a shallow, superficial space, I mean that I've not only seen it in others but have also known it intimately in my own journey. In my career, I've experienced two defining twelve-year cycles that mirrored one another as overarching life lessons. They went something like this: exuberance → performance → disintegration → renewal. I guess I'm a tough case; once wasn't enough!

Straight out of seminary, I launched into the pastorate with my new bride and, although zealous for God and my wife, I promptly displaced both with the mistress of ministry. It's an all-too-common story, and I detail my recovery from it in my first book, *Soul Space*. It took a year's sabbatical in the mountains of Colorado to restore my marriage and my soul, and the reorientation was profound. The crucible had done its refining work, but I was just getting started.

Several years later, a new vision emerged, and I launched my executive-coaching business in 2005. Again, I got off to an exciting, profitable start and experienced a steady upward trend for several years. But although my spiritual practices had deepened, they were not yet strong enough to support my growing influence. Over the next several years, my soul began to flounder.

As the recession hit, business took a dive, and I unconsciously correlated profitability with blessing. Like the girl picking petals off a daisy, saying, "He loves me, he loves me not," my felt experience of God's affection rose and fell with the tides of my profit and loss statement. Through a long series of humiliations, God began to anchor my feet on the bedrock of his unceasing care for me, and I experienced an upswell of gravitas.

In an intensely personal way, I've come to learn that the core truths that comprise our life messages are so precious to God and so fundamental to our callings that many rounds of refining and strengthening are necessary to empower the leadership God intends to bring forth in us. Like layers of an onion, we have to get through one shell to get to the next. In so doing, we pay the price over the course of time and testing to lead with spiritual authority.

This is probably a good time to clarify the sense in which I'm using the expression "spiritual authority." I do *not* mean it to refer to positional authority, such as pastoral staff or the C-suite. Instead, I'm referring to what we've been talking about in these initial pages—*the grace to influence others in redemptive directions by virtue of virtue*, as a result of knowing God deeply and walking with God richly so our influence is inherently God-breathed. This quality often coincides with positional authority yet neither requires it nor can be replaced by it (Matthew 20:25-28).

For illustration, we need not go further than Jesus, a man with little cultural position, yet who continually astounded his listeners, contrasting mightily with the positional authorities of his time: "When Jesus had finished saying these things, the crowds were amazed at his teaching, because he taught *as one who had authority*, and not as their teachers of the law" (Matthew 7:28-29, emphasis added). They seemed even more impressed by the authority he carried in word than in deed; the miracles were the evidence of the authority he carried in his person (Matthew 9:6). And authority was precisely what Jesus bestowed on his disciples as he sent them out to extend what he had begun (Matthew 10:1). Isn't it time for us to live in the fullness of that calling once again?

How Far Is Your Reach?

So it's worth asking, what is the sphere of your spiritual authority? How far is your influence meant to extend? Honestly, most of us don't know—and that's probably by design. If it were further than seems comfortable, we would likely be intimidated . . . and if it were smaller than our ambition, we might well chafe at the constraints. Most of us simply have to live into our destinies one day at a time.

But the reason it's valuable to consider our reach lies in the classic illustration of the branches on a tree. Perhaps you know that the network of roots underneath a tree extend horizontally in roughly the same dimension as the branches.[6] So a tree with a a twenty-foot branch radius, like the weeping cherry in my back-yard, would have a tangle of roots with approximately the same spread beneath the surface. And the towering willow oak just out-side our fence probably has root tendrils that extend almost sixty feet in diameter! *Talk about biological gravitas.*

The influence of leaders can easily outgrow their character. It happens every day. God-engineered giftedness does what it was designed to do: It grows. Branches spread and influence rises. But what was meant for the glory of God is often undermined by a stunted root system, so we now have a leadership landscape virtually littered with capsized "trees," men and women of great potential and calling whose spiritual formation *in* God was cut short in their rush to do great things *for* God, and maybe even somewhat for themselves.

So how far does your leadership influence extend? How many children rely on your spiritual foundation? How many employees or direct reports? How many in your small group? How many represented by the nonprofit board you're on? How many read your books or blog, listen to your podcast, or are on your payroll? Frankly, we have little idea of just how much influence we already carry and are usually naively eager for more.

Now think about the roots underneath your tree. How strong are they, and how deep do they run? Can they sustain a class-7 gale with ease, or do they tremble in a summer thunderstorm? Before you grasp after that next promotion or instigate strategic planning for a new satellite office, it might be time to do some root work.

This book is all about helping you extend your roots, deep and far. It's not about helping you be more externally productive but about helping you thrive internally so that you can fulfill God's greatest purpose through you.

At the same time, you're busy. The pressure for productivity is a constant in your life. Is rootedness worth the time? In Jesus' words, "Come . . . and you will see" (John 1:39).

If you're ready to grow your gravitas, come join those who have gone before. Let's learn from the monastics how to go more deep than wide. We don't have to be the spiritual elite; all we need is desire . . . because that is precisely where God meets us and does extraordinary things. Let's get started.

1
SPIRITUAL GRAVITAS

Not Going Wide but Going Deep

---

*Let us rouse ourselves from lethargy. . . . Let us open our eyes to
the light that can change us into the likeness of God. Let our ears
be alert to the stirring call of his voice crying to us every day.*

RULE OF ST. BENEDICT, prologue

TINA IS THE FOUNDER AND CEO of a global-missions agency that
provides coaching and training for cross-cultural leaders around
the world. Her organization equips leaders as they prepare for
service, walks with them as they work in host countries, and then
supports them as they cross cultures again upon their return home.
She is very good at what she does.

Tina came to me for two reasons: She wanted to write a career-
defining book, and she was seriously overextended. She might not
have been in burnout, but she was certainly getting crispy around
the edges. And her two coaching agendas held an ironic tension
between them.

The cause of her overextension was as ubiquitous as her title:
a tightly stretched calendar, overtaxed budgets, highly complex

planning for overseas events, frayed-edge relationships. Dilemmas landed on her desk more quickly than solutions could be generated, multiplying pressure and frustration. In short, she was spread broad and shallow. Her "branches" had overextended her "roots," and intuitively, she knew it.

Eight months later—after a host of conversations shared, pages written, and spiritual practices employed—I started to hear different words from Tina: words like *happier, relaxed, less pressure, a wider perspective.* We continued to work together for another couple of years as both her book and her soul took healthier shape. Tina's leadership challenges never lessened, but she was better able to support them as she deepened her roots and laid serious boundaries against overextension—not unlike some of our biblical mentors. Let's take a look.

Overextension and Redemption

Moses got a crash course on overextension when his leadership gifts were activated without the character to sustain them. As a Hebrew raised in the Egyptian court of Pharaoh, he intervened against the oppression of his fellow Israelites. But he did so without the benefit of gravitas: He lost his temper and killed a man . . . and lost the chance to exert the influence God had planned for him as a national leader. The roots were shallow, and the tree came down. Fortunately, God's habit of redeeming our blunders brought Moses back around to the same calling forty years later, when his roots had grown out substantially.

It's worth noting that when it comes to spiritual gravitas, Moses carried some serious weight in his second career. Power confrontations with Pharaoh, parting a sea, and bringing water out of a rock are just a few of the evidences of his genuine spiritual authority. But my favorite shows up at the conclusion of a mountaineering expedition, when Moses returned from a God encounter and his face was physically glowing (Exodus 34:29-35). A visible light emanated from the pores of his skin as manifestation of the presence of God that rested on him. I'd call that spiritual authority. How about you?

Many years later, when Israel occupied the Promised Land, the nation was ruled by judges. One of the most powerful of these was a woman named Deborah. She carried immense authority, particularly in that patriarchal culture, and was, first and foremost, a judicial leader who settled disputes that naturally arose among the tribes. Later she was a military leader who inspired courage and laid out strategy when the heart of the nation had fallen to a low ebb. Her gravitas led to a forty-year peace for her people (Judges 4–5).

Many years later again, similar spiritual weight captured great attention in the wake of Peter and John's testimony before the Sanhedrin. Having just healed a man and preached to a large crowd, much to the chagrin of the Jewish power base, these two disciples were dragged into court to give an account for themselves. The author Luke records that "when they saw the courage of Peter and John and realized that they were unschooled, ordinary men, they were astonished and they took note that these men had been with Jesus" (Acts 4:13).

Authority by Proximity

What was true then is still true now: *Concentrated amounts of time in the presence of God change us.* Ancient spiritual practices transform our character and anchor us in a heavenly reality that shines out of us, either physically or metaphysically, with spiritual authority. This spiritual afterglow is not for ego or entertainment; instead, it opens a channel for God to do what God wants to do. That's the bottom line. God's redemptive agenda is facilitated by men and women who have been with Jesus and who carry his authority.

Among the women and men I coach, I hear a desire for *not more breadth but more depth*, not more tasks and responsibilities but the chance to do a better job at what they're already juggling. They yearn for a sense of rootedness that stabilizes the soul in the midst of chaos. Jesus described a house built on solid rock in a well-known story: Its foundations ran so deep and strong that a veritable hurricane couldn't dislodge it (Matthew 7:24-25). Stormproof leadership is deep-rooted, not overextended.

The ultimate spiritual gravitas was carried, of course, by Jesus himself. And of the many examples we could look at, we'll tag just one for now. Jesus was nearing the Crucifixion and had wrestled with God in prayer all night. As the eastern sky lightened ever so slightly, Judas the betrayer led a detachment of soldiers to place Jesus under arrest. Arriving with torches blazing and swords drawn, they were an intimidating force; it was a scary time for the disciples.

John is the only Gospel that records this particular account of Jesus' force of presence. "Who is it you want?" Jesus asked. "Jesus of Nazareth," they replied. *A pregnant pause.* "I am he" was his simple reply . . . but as these words crossed Jesus' lips, the entire detachment of battle-hardened soldiers "drew back and fell to the ground" (John 18:4-6). Wow. That was some serious juice.

I doubt any of us are looking for a spiritual force field that knocks people down . . . Well, I take that back. In some meetings, that could come in handy! But certainly we *are* looking for a strength of leadership that goes far beyond the best practices of the secular sphere. We need more than Gallup polls and industry trends, more than power talks and power naps and power ties and power lunches. As useful as those may be, we need something rock-solid under our feet.

We need the daily life force of God flowing in our veins, rocking our worlds, infusing our minds with wisdom and our souls with joy, stormproofing our minds and anchoring our convictions with monk-like serenity and compassion.

The Cost of Spiritual Gravitas

This kind of leadership substance cannot be announced in a press release; it must be felt. It cannot be rushed or faked; it must be earned. "Earning" is funny language to use in the realm of the Spirit, where mercy rules and personal performance falls ridiculously short of divine love, a love that cannot be increased or diminished. God's delight in us and commitment to us is gratuitous. Unceasing. Unearnable.

But some things are not bestowed; they are paid for in blood, sweat, and tears. Think about honor. Trust. Integrity. Character. And yes, spiritual authority. These commodities carry a price tag, one that not all leaders are prepared to pay. True gravitas is egoless, and the journey to that particular freedom is arduous for all of us. We typically have to reach and fall, then reach and land through many iterations of God's patient, gentle invitation toward a life of love. *Love is both the beginning and the end of trustworthy spiritual leadership.*

Even Jesus had to earn his spiritual authority. Remember? He laid aside the divine power he carried in heaven to enter earth (Philippians 2:6-8). Commissioned by Father and Spirit in a river baptism, he was sent immediately into the proving ground of the desert (Matthew 4:1-11). If anyone should get a free pass on gravitas, I think it would be Jesus . . . but even here, the roots must go down in the epicenter of the storm. And a fierce storm it was. Weakened physically from lack of food and water, Jesus faced three temptations that all leaders must face. See if you recognize them.

The spiritual writer Henri Nouwen describes these three with artful precision: the temptation to be *relevant* (turning stones into bread), the temptation to be *spectacular* (leaping off the Temple), and the temptation to be *powerful* (taking control of human wealth and rule).[1]

What's so wrong with being relevant or powerful . . . or even spectacular? On the face of it, nothing. But underneath the surface, something fundamental is being established: the *source* of Jesus' gravitas. Even the Son of God had to relinquish his human authority in order to participate in the divine life—as do we (2 Peter 1:3-4).

We will return to this scene again, but until we, too, pass these tests as leaders, we will be spiritually untrustworthy, attempting to do good things with fatally flawed motivations. Yes, there is a cost for spiritual authority, but the return on investment is huge. Without divine authority, all we're left with is human power, and even when well-intentioned, that tends to generate collateral damage.

Character that goes the distance doesn't come by happenstance; it comes by enduring the hard places . . . for a long time

. . . without quitting. Paul said it this way: "We also glory in our sufferings, because we know that suffering produces perseverance; perseverance, character; and character, hope. And hope does not put us to shame, because God's love has been poured out into our hearts through the Holy Spirit, who has been given to us" (Romans 5:3-5). Men and women of spiritual gravitas have character with deep roots, birthed by persevering through difficulty and marked by profound hope. And, I might add, joy.

So the theory is good, and the biblical model is sound. We want to be this kind of leader. We don't want to be double-minded, self-doubting; we don't want to choke in the clutch. We don't want to be "blown and tossed by the wind," as James described those without adequate character (James 1:6). We want to be a rock of strength, calm under fire. We want to inspire and equip those who look to us. We want to advance the purposes of God on the earth. *But how?*

Seriously, how do we do this?

A Road Map for Gravitas

To become modern monks, we now turn to the ancients. Of the many monastic orders that influenced the world for good, one stands out in its construction, its longevity, and its impact: the Benedictines.

It was roughly AD 480 when Benedict was born, the son of a nobleman who seemed destined for a life of leisure and affluence. Instead, at about the age of twenty, Benedict became disillusioned with the meaninglessness of it all, left his studies in Rome, and traveled forty miles east to the mountain town of Enfide. There he discovered a cave overlooking a lake, where he proceeded to live as a hermit for the next three years, growing his character in a place of solitude.

Benedict was invited to become the abbot of a nearby monastery in Subiaco, where he spent the next few years enduring the territorialism and hostility of neighboring monks before leaving to form twelve of his own monasteries in the region. He eventually founded the great monastery of Monte Cassino in AD 529 on a hilltop between Rome and Naples. This gentle monk is often considered the founder of western monasticism due to the influence of his spiritual authority and his writings on the spiritual life.

The Benedictines are famous for their "Rule of Life," a written set of principles and practices that anchored their lives and ordered their ministry. Over the course of this book, you will be invited to rough out some of the principles and practices on which you will base your leadership in the coming years. Don't be intimidated by this: It can be as simple or elaborate as you wish. What's important is that it flows out of your own earnest inquiry and that the practices help you become and remain the most authentic version of yourself, the woman or man God knows you can be and is inviting you to become.

The Secrets of the Monastery

Those who joined the Benedictine order had to take three vows and commit themselves to five specific practices. These will form the structure for our conversation in this book; the upcoming chapters will track with those vows (or principles) and the practices that flow out of those vows. We will look briefly at what these commitments might have meant in their time and then, more importantly, how to live in the spirit of these principles and practices in ways that speak to the pressing needs of our immediate world.

On a practical note, the term *monk* will be used gender-inclusively in this book, as befits the Greek origins of the word (*monachos*). In modern times, the word *nun* is often used to refer to women monastics, but all the principles we will explore in this book apply equally to both women and men. And while our context will be largely around leadership roles, the spiritual practices I suggest will deepen and enrich the lives of anyone.

If, like me, you are a Protestant, I encourage you to open your heart to a tradition that may feel foreign. The monastic heritage predates most of the church divisions that must now grieve the heart of God (John 17:20-23). I grew up in a charismatic, nondenominational, low-church, highly contemporary spiritual tradition, and in the years since, I have worshiped with a wide array of denominational gatherings. The practices described by Benedict are as theologically orthodox and centrist as any you'll find, although in places you'll also find them wrapped in ancient language that may be new to you.

At this point in the chapter, you may feel inspired but also a little daunted. Don't be. *Your spiritual formation is not merely another set of tasks for your to-do list!* It is a fundamental change to your way of being in the world, and the result—I hope—is that your to-do list will have less tyranny over your life.

If you are a business owner or a business manager, this is your chance. Get ready to put down some roots. If you are a pastor or a ministry leader, get ready to deepen your character and connect more strongly with God. In years past, marketplace leaders often looked to ministry leaders to show them the way. These days, ministry leaders are often infatuated with secular models of leadership and have largely lost the spiritual authority to model the gravitas needed in today's world. Secular models of leadership do indeed offer important practical insights, and we should take advantage of them. But we cannot help contemporary society reclaim its soul without something more powerful and enduring. To become modern monks in the marketplace, we must go deep in order to lead large.

Relinquishing Our Programs for Happiness

Going deep invites us to come to terms with a cluster of vulnerabilities we all share—three instincts that touch our deepest human longings: *control, affection,* and *security.* This orientation is so pervasive in the human journey that we will return to it again and again. Let's dig into it right here at the beginning.

A large chunk of our words, attitudes, and behaviors flows directly out of one of these three motivations: We try to power up in situations to avoid feeling out of control; we reach discretely to earn approval and affection from those whose opinions we value; we create agendas (seen and unseen) to feel more safe and secure in an unpredictable world. This is not some of us; this is all of us.

It was a modern monk, Thomas Keating, who coined the expression "emotional programs for happiness" to describe our human instincts toward meeting these legitimate needs in illegitimate ways.[2] He observed these three tendrils and then described how they creep into our behavior as vain efforts to be happy. We all want to be happy. And the lack of control, affection, and security feels noticeably unhappy!

What is fascinating to me is how each of the Benedictine vows confronts one of these programs of human longing with divine supply. We long for these three qualities in our lives (one in particular, based on our personality) not because they are bad but because they are good. The quandary comes when we cannot generate them for ourselves—and we never really can.

No matter how much we posture and jockey for power (even in our own lives, not to mention in others' lives), when are we ever really in full control? And how much power do we wield to make people like us? The best we can do is try to please, but even here, there is no guarantee of affection. And security? Come on! Even the wealthiest can't buy safety from so many of life's threats. So it's right here that the effervescent happiness that we find in Jesus attests to the impact of the gospel: *We don't have to!* We don't have to spin our wheels in desperate efforts to be safe, loved, and strong because God has already offered those gratuitously. Free and clear. On the house. We can't generate them; we can only receive them.

What an incredible relief.

Our emotional programs for happiness get triggered in a big way as we attempt to compensate for our human fragility. And this is where personality takes on distinct form: We criticize others or we criticize ourselves. We work harder or we play harder. We try to solve it in our heads or connect with it in our hearts or bodies. We try to be more different or we try to be more the same. We get angry or fearful or deceptive or aloof as a way of feeling stronger, safer, and more lovable.

There are religious versions of this too. We can subconsciously inflate our spiritual persona. We can subtly (or not so subtly) announce our achievements, responsibilities, or busyness. We can flatter or demand. We can withhold knowledge or intrude with it. We can use overtly spiritual language to buffer our personal agendas. But none of these strategies work; they do not make us happier. Even when they appear to work, it's an illusion. And the illusion of generating our own happiness is perhaps the greatest danger of all.

So what if you and I don't have to control the people and appearances and circumstances of life? The only way that could be true is if God really has all things under control—the good, the bad, and the ugly all belong and serve their purpose. Dare we believe that? And what if we are all ultimately safe—not from pain or tragedy but in the midst of it? What if God's commitment to our good cannot be compromised by any flaw in ourselves or in others, cannot be unbroken by loss of job or spouse or money or even life itself? Well, that would be security indeed. And what if approval and affection were ours for the taking, unlimited in scope and degree?

Receiving what we crave most around these three needs hinges on two things: our view of God and our view of God's view of us. Is God pleased or angry? Is God merciful or vindictive? Despite all sound theology, it's more likely than not that we experience a vague sense of God's pleasure in those rare moments when we've got all our plates spinning as impressively as possible—and a vague sense of God's disappointment in those more common moments when the plates begin to topple; when we're not getting our devotions in regularly; when we're not getting to the gym regularly; when we're not making it to Bible study regularly; when dinner is burned and the kids are crying and the lawn isn't mowed. How does God feel about us then?

Only a clear eye toward God's unmitigated delight in us has the capacity to evoke the abiding experience of approval, security, and control that we need in our depths. Our ability to feel approved by

God, to feel the security of his embrace, and to entrust ourselves to his control—each of these depends on our view of God.

Wow, can you feel your roots going down even as we consider these profound truths? This is a groundedness beyond expectation. This is where gravitas begins.

Even though we are going to explore the monastics, we don't live cloistered lives: We live in the thick of life, which is exactly where God's ways are needed most. But we can't carry something we don't have, and that takes us to our own personal monastery—the space where we cultivate our awareness of God and of God's transforming grace in our lives through spiritual practice.

INTO THE MONASTERY

Each chapter ends with an invitation into the sacred space of solitude by suggesting exercises in personal reflection, evaluation, practice, or refocus. For now, simply jot down some thoughts around the following questions:

1. What are the most perplexing challenges confronting my leadership today?

2. What connections do I see between spiritual depth and marketplace effectiveness?

3. How would I evaluate my current spiritual authority?

4. If I were mentoring a new leader, what spiritual practices would I suggest for the development of his or her "root system"?

IN COMMUNITY

One of the gifts of the monastery is *community*. As a young man, Benedict left a very secure world of status to seek a more spiritual center to his life. He spent the next three years living alone in a cave, deepening his own spiritual roots. But although Benedict was no stranger to solitude, his passion was to cultivate community—to create a spiritually rich environment where monks could live and learn and grow together over the years.

Similarly, you will glean the most from your journey through this book if you are in a small community that focuses on this purpose—perhaps a small group that already enjoys fellowship together or one where you gather specifically for this reason. At the least, invite one close spiritual friend to share the journey with you. The benefits are numerous if you think about it.

- *Disclosure is intrinsically formative.* Transparency—honesty with yourself and honesty with trusted others—is the first prerequisite for personal transformation. It's pretty tough to grow your soul and your practice without naming your current condition in a safe place. Together with others who are eager for leadership formation, you can walk the road in community.

- *Companionship strengthens resolve.* Isolation makes for easy pickings, but like-minded friends can guard one another's backs. It's just too easy to get confused, frustrated, and disillusioned when we're in it alone. The solidarity that comes from true companions on the journey is priceless.

- *Conversation broadens insight.* Transformation is more than practice; awareness and learning take place most powerfully in conversation. Often it's not until we share our experiences—both obstacles and successes—that revelation is kindled, insights are confirmed, and roots are formed.

So the person (or group) I'd like to invite to join me in my exploration of gravitas is . . .

2

STABILITY

Not Pushing the Envelope but Feeling the Love

---

*When the decision is made that novices are to be accepted, then
they come before the whole community in the oratory to make [a]
solemn promise of stability, fidelity to monastic life and obedience.*

RULE OF ST. BENEDICT, chapter 58

IT WAS A BRIGHT, WARM APRIL DAY in 2009 when Dan and I
sat down to talk for the first time. "I'm a good pastor and a
good preacher," Dan said, "but after ten years, I still have
trouble finding joy. I often dream about doing something else
but fear I would be stepping out of God's will." As the conversation deepened, I felt his uncertainty and instability as a visceral
force. I also sensed his deep integrity and sincere desire to lead
people well.

In the months that followed, we went through a host of exercises
together to augment the discernment process: lists of drainers and
energizers (75 percent felt draining!), discussion of family stresses,
exploration of life purpose and calling, and a candid assessment of
career alternatives. We also dug down into his spiritual practices;

while he was faithful in prayer and Bible reading, he admitted that he rarely took time off from work. Ministry felt like a twenty-four-seven obligation, but he was motivated to incorporate a true Sabbath—and to finally get serious about his dwindling health and expanding waistline.

Dan was focused and motivated. Over the next two years, he made many changes: He cut himself loose from the youth ministry. He embraced the teaching role that energized him. He orchestrated a church survey and instigated overdue shifts within the life of the church. He lost weight and increased time in the gym. But it was something else entirely that opened the door of his emerging clarity and stability: more spacious time in God's presence, space that opened his soul to experiencing more of God's love for him personally.

The journey was bumpy, with steps forward and steps back. But ultimately, the experience of being cared for deeply by God revealed his path forward. Staff changed, church culture changed, and positions were realigned, and Dan settled happily back into a new groove in the same church. After several years of turbulence, stability returned. Dan stayed and thrived.

Living Off Balance

We live in a world of constant change. A world where everything is disposable. Diapers, silverware, gloves—all disposable now. Even cell phones and printers are usually cheaper to replace than repair. And relationships—well, those often feel disposable too. When a dispute arises or feelings get hurt, whether it's with your dentist or your boss or your pastor, it's easier to leave than to fix it. America is the land of forty-seven brands of breakfast cereal, and we are here to be inspired and entertained. When I get tired of how you "taste," it's as easy as picking up a new brand. What a great life.

Or not.

The fracture lines across marriages and churches and communities at large attest to the fact that we are relationally challenged and that for all our easy outs, we simply carry the same dysfunctions into the next context without experiencing much in the way of true transformation. I know I have. I've done my share of cutting bait and running, abandoning close friendships, drifting from casual ones, and fleeing spiritual leaders who no longer felt trustworthy. Yes, I've done my share of leaving, unaware of the incisive wisdom of a monk named Benedict who lived and taught and led 1,500 years ago.

As Benedict found others drawn to his spiritual leadership, and after experiencing a number of enormously dysfunctional spiritual communities (including one where a monastic leader actually tried to poison him!), he began to imagine what it would take to create a healthy environment for people to love God and one another for the long run. And he came up with three qualities that would be required of every novice monk to become part of his community: *stability*, *conversion*, and *obedience*. Of all the potential commitments Benedict could have selected for his monastery, he chose these three—and required a "solemn promise . . . before God and the saints" to remain faithful to these three virtues above all.[1]

In our first few chapters, we will unpack these three vows, starting with the commitment to stability. For Benedict's initial community—as well as for the thousands of communities that sprung up in his wake and continue to this day—the promise to lead a life of stability was anchored in a very sobering practicality: that whatever specific community these new monks joined, they would remain there for life! Now that's a serious commitment, one that makes me just a little jittery. In the modern Western world, we have little reference for such an enduring commitment; the only thing that even comes close is marriage . . . and we can see how well *that's* going across the nation.

The wider priority, if we're to judge by what we see, is an enduring commitment to getting ahead. Pushing the envelope is the unspoken vow of most in the modern workplace. Pushing for more recognition, more power, more income. So while all of these things can be used for good, they also feed our egos—and *ego is one of the greatest threats to our spiritual authority*. Ego and force of will do not equip us to bring God's purposes into our world. No, we need something deeper, truer, more anchored.

What we want to explore here is how the concept and experience of stability applies today for those of us who have landed far from the monastery in the thick of life and leadership. If it's not a quaint stone castle we're committing ourselves to, what exactly should it be? WWBD: *What would Benedict do?*

It will be your job to answer that question—not for Benedict, of course, but for yourself, in your life and your world. And you'll have a place to do just that at the end of each chapter. If there is no modern practical application to these ancient virtues, then we're wasting our time here. I am convinced, however, that there are very practical, very personal, and very transformational applications for each of us—opportunities to put spiritual roots down deep and discover a powerful new way of living and leading that brings new solutions to old problems (or, should we say, old solutions to new problems). To open the conversation, I'll share an account of how stability recently enriched my journey.

Fight or Flight or . . . Simply Stay

It was December of 2010 when I sat down at Starbucks to meet
Cindy Mondello, the executive director of Restoration Place
Counseling. Drawn together by mutual friends, we quickly connected over our shared passion for life restoration, to which Cindy
had devoted herself in the form of counseling hurting women
through every kind of life trauma you can imagine. Inspired by her
commitment and impressed by the ministry's track record, I didn't
hesitate when she asked me to join the organizational development
committee. And so a very meaningful relationship and ministry
partnership began.

Three years later, however, I was ready to take my marbles and
go home.

A year on committee had led to a year on the board, which
led to accepting the board chair position for 2013. I sat down at
the board retreat that January with a bit of a rush, anticipating all
that we might accomplish together. I opened the meeting with
an inspiring story, overviewed the last several years of dramatic
growth, and cast an aggressive vision for doubling client capacity
over the coming year. I could tell the team was with me; the energy
was palpable. This was going to be fun.

Ten months later, a series of "burs under my saddle" were
starting to wear raw, and I felt myself pulling away from Cindy.
A relatively small disagreement about fee pricing brought things
to a head that December, and I wrestled over whether to remain
on the board into the new year. I didn't feel great about staying,
but I didn't feel peace about leaving. Taking my ambivalence to
prayer, all I heard was "wait."

I eased gingerly into the new year, remaining on the board

but no longer the chair, feeling disengaged but honoring the only direction I had, which was to simply stay put. It was painful for me, and I think it was at least a little painful for Cindy. Although we had said the right words to clear the air in December, the distance remained. It was awkward at best.

Several monthly meetings down the road, I noticed that I was no longer dreading the board gatherings; instead I entered the room with clear eyes and a less-guarded attitude. Cindy and I smiled cautiously at each other and started to get back to work. I found myself wondering, *What was that all about? What changed?* Eventually, the truth of the matter dawned on me with a jolt: *We resolved our relational tension by staying in relationship.* Could it really be that simple?

Some Modern Faces of Stability

Stability *is* simple, although its application can take various faces. Let's explore a few of the faces of stability and why they might be important for modern leaders.

Relational Stability

The story I shared of my experience with Cindy speaks to the relational application of stability, which is bigger than we know. Discarded relationships tear quietly at the fabric of our souls, eating into the larger connectedness we're meant to share in life—and the stability that such communal foundations are meant to provide. This slow erosion takes a higher toll on spiritual authority than we often realize.

There are, of course, legitimate reasons to step away from dysfunctional relationships, particularly when abusive dynamics are at play and the power differential is tilted in favor of the abuser. In our human finiteness, not all relationships can be repaired. Nor do all parties want health and healing; sometimes people are committed to their dysfunctions, and sometimes, those people are us! But it takes little to brand someone as toxic and check out. In our current milieu, we are more apt to leave too early than stay too long.

For myself, the tendency to pull away from ailing relationships stems most often from a lack of courage—*reticence to engage in hard conversations with honesty and kindness.* So I sacrifice one on the altar of the other: Usually, I'll choose a dishonest kindness; occasionally, I'll choose an unkind honesty. But amazing things happen when we extend both at the same time. This bold play opens the door for redemption, and that is the very breath of heaven.

There are other reasons to avoid staying put in relationships, motivations that flow out of different personality styles. But to the extent that we can do the hard work of engaging the people we live, work, and worship with, we stabilize our world and the world of others. This relational groundedness begins in the home with the family and ripples out in all directions from there.

This progression is worthy of special note for leaders. The weight of responsibility that leaders carry outside the home, along with the addictive nature of work itself, stack the deck of priority—and it's usually the family that suffers for it. Because we leave for work every day, it's easy for that leaving to creep into the essence of relationship itself, with collateral damage to spouses and children. We must find creative ways to be faithful to our vocations without injuring those closest to us. Their stability as well as ours depends on it; it's part of our spiritual authority and our most central responsibility.

The commitment to stability calls us toward the reality of God's eternal Kingdom, where community will be unbroken by human frailty. We get powerful glimpses of this from John the Revelator, who peered into the worship of heaven, where "every nation, tribe, people and language" was gathered in perfect fellowship (Revelation 7:9). No one leaves; no one wants to. This is where we're headed, so let's get ready now.

Geographical Stability

Recently, I've become intrigued by the spiritual ramifications of holding stable within a physical area; of remaining within a city or region for long periods of time—maybe even a lifetime. This is, of course, foreign to our day and age, even though you don't have to go back many generations to find that as the norm.

I was in an exercise class at the YMCA a little while ago when another person in the same class connected the dots and realized we had gone to high school together across the state thirty years prior! Over those years, I have lived in three different communities (not counting college). I was stunned to hear that since high school, she hasn't been in the same location for more than three years: She's lived in more than ten communities across the nation and the world in thirty years! I found myself wondering what the internal consequences of such geographic instability might be. As Carole King laments in song, "Doesn't anybody stay in one place anymore?"[2]

Of course, there are legitimate reasons to move across the country or the world. Vocational development may send us, family connections may call us, divine intrusions may redirect us. We just need to understand that there may be unseen spiritual dimensions in play.

I have to note the irony that, as I write this, I have just moved geographies myself after fourteen years. There are reasons—good ones and even relational ones—but I'm curious whether such a move comes with a hit on the gravitas tank. The Benedictines believed that a lifetime spent in a single geography had serious spiritual impact. In fact, the ancient world prioritized geography by building it into people's names: Saul of Tarsus, Augustine of Hippo, Benedict of Nursia. Perhaps it's time we at least consider the effects of geographical stability versus transience.

Internal Stability

Of all the applications of stability we might consider in the modern world, perhaps none hit as close to home as stability of soul: the ability to weather the storms of intimidation, the waves of ego, and the gales of unforeseen circumstance.

These three subcomponents of stability—there are no doubt others—interpenetrate one another. How many of our relationships do we carry with us in any meaningful way from one geography to the next? On the whole, very few. Often the only connection we have with those from past geographies is the annual Christmas card; meanwhile we start building new relationships from scratch.

New relationships bring new opportunities, yet the time to lay foundations that can sustain deep relational connection cannot be rushed. A one-year friendship, no matter how dear to us, cannot match the depth of a ten-year friendship that has been cultivated and sustained across the mountains and valleys of circumstances.

An active thirty-year friendship is priceless. And these are formed, or at least influenced, by geography.

My recent move to the mountains of North Carolina, from a place of long-cultivated relationships to a place of almost none, rocked me internally. The geography was familiar, having imprinted itself on my young soul during childhood vacations to my grandfather's place, so I wasn't entirely prepared for the internal vertigo of the move. And there was only one prescription for healing this malady: time. Time to put new roots down in a new sphere of community.

How we need a rock of internal stability from which to exercise our leadership. Gravitas is forged from such stability, creating men and women of substance. Are you one of them? Am I?

Jesus painted a compelling scene that we alluded to earlier:

> Everyone who hears these words of mine and *puts them into practice* is like a wise man who built his house on the rock. The rain came down, the streams rose, and the winds blew and beat against that house; yet it did not fall, because it had its foundation on the rock. But everyone who hears these words of mine *and does not put them into practice* is like a foolish man who built his house on sand. The rain came down, the streams rose, and the winds blew and beat against that house, and it fell with a great crash.
>
> MATTHEW 7:24-27, EMPHASIS ADDED

Pressure. Stress. Uncertainty. Risk. They are part of life and amplified for leaders. What about you—how do you carry them? Do you fake it till you make it? Do you internalize them? Externalize them? Ride them?

Jesus highlighted the tipping point from sand to rock with a single word: *practice*. It's what we might call *doing what you know to do*. Not intelligence . . . although smart leaders are people of action. Not experience . . . although seasoned leaders are often marked by such integrity. Not charisma or timing or market savvy or any of a long list of other potential assets. Those who hold steady in the storm are those who have cultivated a life of practice, and for our purposes, I'll zero in on spiritual practices.

We all live, every one of us, with some degree of gap between what we *want* to do and what we *actually* do. Those who become monks in the marketplace aren't those who have eliminated the gap but those who pay attention to the gap. They have filtered out the noise of culture enough to "hear these words" of Kingdom import and have created a personal rhythm that places spiritual practices at the very core of life—and at the center of leadership. These are not things we do when time and space make it convenient, nor things we do at the break of day so we can get on with the real business of the day. These are practices that *form a container to hold the day*. This is what roots look like, and it's where we're headed in the coming chapters.

Challenging a Culture of Urgency

Let's be candid. Ours is a culture of urgency. We have an ethos of drivenness fueled by thinly veiled terror and less-veiled ambition. This is how we push the envelope. Even baptized in Christian language and godly objective, *ambition is still ultimately about us* once we pare it down to the naked truth: *our* desire to be significant, our need to be needed. Yeah, painful as it is to admit, all our work for God in the world—and I mean all of it—is shot through with all-too-human angst. It's part of the package, and God has never been surprised or stymied by the extent of it.

Robert Mulholland describes it as the difference between being "*in the world for God*" and being "*in God for the world*."[3] Quite a difference, huh? Can you feel that pull, that "deep call[ing] to deep" (Psalm 42:7) of God's desire to be with you echoed in your own desire for God? Or maybe you feel conflicted, part of you drawn in and another part wondering if it's worth the effort.

I was consulting with a sharp leader in a large Christian ministry, asking questions to elicit the corporate culture of their international enterprise. "Our ministry is marked by urgency," he intoned. "The world has yet to be evangelized, and we may only have a few generations left. So we work hard and long to get the job done." And from conversations I'd had with other team members, I knew he was telling the truth! The pace was frantic. Burnout was endemic. Everything was done with excellence, but thousands of dedicated men and women were paying a high price. Too high, in my opinion.

The unquestioned value of urgency is rife within contemporary society, driven largely by fear and greed. It's ridiculously easy to import this culture of urgency into Kingdom work, knowing that at least we're applying our efforts toward eternal results rather than temporal ones. Like Jesus, we are "about [our] Father's business" (Luke 2:49, NKJV), but are we doing business *the way Jesus did it*?

Jesus and Stability

Maybe it's just me, but when I look at the life of Jesus spread across four Gospel accounts, I see a lot of values in motion, *but urgency isn't one of them.* For starters, let's consider one monumental truth: Out of thirty-three years on the planet, Jesus doesn't start his ministry—doesn't preach his first sermon or heal his first disease—until year thirty. That's like entering your office to start the workday at 5:00 p.m. and leaving at 6:00 p.m. If we're simply looking at a divine to-do list, it's not exactly a study in urgency!

Once Jesus does get into ministry gear, he's playing sommelier at a wedding party, inviting himself to dinner with IRS agents, and having his feet washed awkwardly at a Pharisee dinner. Then he's multiplying food for flash mobs. All I can say is, there's a whole lot of eating and drinking going on around Jesus, which really bugged the Jewish rabbis. And even though I'm having some fun with this, maybe you get my point by noticing *what's not there* in Jesus' three years of active ministry.

We don't see Jesus doing strategic planning with the disciples: "First we saturate Capernaum because that's the low-hanging fruit. Once we hit the focus-group goal of seventy disciples, we launch satellite campuses as regional cost centers . . ." And we don't see Jesus attempting to build momentum, which is what every modern enterprise prizes most. Astoundingly, he pulled back as soon as the crowds hit a critical mass.

Jesus sabotages growth constantly by telling healed people not to advertise. He intentionally obfuscates his message and offends his best customers. He goes out of his way to antagonize local governance. He breaks every rule and convention, particularly the ones that would guarantee commercial success, much to the consternation of his executive team.

But above all, Jesus never seems to be in a hurry—even when he should be, like when his best friend is dying! Jesus moves deliberately, slowly even, and seems to have time for every interruption

(John 11:1-7). Clearly, Jesus is operating from a different set of values than ours. Are we paying attention?

Purposeful: yes. Urgent: no.

So what does that have to do with stability? Just this: *Soul stability and urgency are incompatible.* If stability is to become a virtue that empowers your leadership effectiveness and spiritual gravitas, urgency has got to go! Focus, accountability, teamwork, courage, endurance—all these culture qualities you'll see reflected in the Master Leader. But desperate motivational tirades, frantic sprints to deadlines, clenched jaws, and hand-wringing—not so much. So why do we do these things? Why do we accept them without question as the price of leadership, even the trophy of leadership?

In their place, you'll observe in Jesus a remarkable composure and internal stability, even in the face of circumstantial turbulence and outright hostility. If there's one story that just nails it for me, it's when Jesus suggested to his disciples that they sail across the Sea of Galilee from Capernaum to the region of the Gerasenes, a jaunt of about five nautical miles. It must have taken a while, because the long day caught up with him, and Jesus found a spot to lean back and take a nap—and remained asleep even when the wind whipped up and the chop began to crest the gunwales. The disciples weren't just annoyed; they were panicked and angry that Jesus wasn't panicking too. Jesus woke up, saw the genuine threat to the group, and solved the problem (Mark 4:35-41). Supernaturally, yes. But the miracle is less the point than Jesus' *way of being* in a time of crisis. His groundedness, his stability is the moral of the story . . . and a compelling call to our own leadership in a season of storms.

Belovedness as Stability

What these revelations would do for us, in addition to rerouting our failed attempts at generating our own happiness, is establish the one thing each of us needs most: *a stable identity.* An unshakable sense of self, grounded in our own skin and in our own world, anchored deep beneath all merit and performance. What would that be like? Can we even imagine?

Look how God established this fundamental identity in Jesus and how Jesus got it! Maybe we can follow suit.

Picture a cloudless morning as the sun begins to warm the rocky Israeli soil, and the shallow waters of the Jordan River run cool and inviting. John the Baptizer holds the crowd rapt with attention, some in admiration and others in contempt. Suddenly he falls strangely silent, staring across the clumps of onlookers and catching sight of his cousin Jesus. Something moves deeply within him, and he calls Jesus over.

After a minor disagreement about who should be baptizing whom, John accepts the request and baptizes Jesus in the river. As Jesus comes up out of the water, a holy hush falls as the people see a mystical manifestation of the Spirit resting birdlike on his head and then hear the divine voice speaking consummate approval: "This is My beloved Son, in whom I am well-pleased" (Matthew 3:17, NASB). *Beloved Son. Well-pleased.* Aren't those words captivating? Can you hear them spoken over you? A friend of mine recently told me, "I can accept the *beloved Son* part, but I really struggle over the *well-pleased* part because I don't think I'm really pleasing God all that often."

But consider this: How many miracles has Jesus performed yet? How many demons has he cast out at this point? How many parables has he told and cripples has he healed? Zero. None. Nada. Jesus hasn't even gotten out of the gate in his ministry yet, but Father God is absolutely delighted in him already! And being delighted in is Jesus' "secret weapon," his *being* from which all his *doing* flows.

At one point in his ministry, Jesus takes advantage of a quiet moment with his disciples to draw out their understanding of his identity, asking, "Who do you say that I am?" Getting it right this time, Peter famously replies, "You are the Christ, the Son of the living God" (Matthew 16:15-16, NASB). We're so used to using the term *Christ* as a singular title for a singular man that it's easy to lose sight of the literal meaning of the word: "anointed." So, anointed with what? In his earthly journey, Jesus is anointed literally with perfume and figuratively with many things, including authority and suffering. But his first anointing is with water and blessing in the Jordan. In other words, Peter gets a divine revelation of Jesus' true identity: *You are the Son of God, anointed with favor. You are the Beloved!*

After the disciples awaken to Jesus' secret of living as the Beloved, God puts an exclamation point on it six days later at the Mount of Transfiguration, where he repeats his original identity statement over Jesus: "This is My beloved Son, with whom I am well-pleased" (Matthew 17:5, NASB). I imagine God thinking, *Are you getting it? Guys, this "beloved child" conviction is Jesus' core reality, the source of his anointing, and I want it to be yours too.*

Elsewhere, Jesus told a crowd a story about a prodigal son, attempting to convey this same truth by parable. Before leaving home, the prodigal enjoys all the provision of the father, but he doesn't enjoy the father. Somehow he has lost his beloved-son identity, and as a result, he loses all sense of direction and purpose. Humbled by the storms of life, he returns to find that the father's love inexplicably remains. Favor flows without any reference to his bad behavior. So the son steps back into his beloved-son identity. Why wouldn't he? And why wouldn't we? Tragically the older son never does discover this reality, so he lives a cramped, bitter life; despite being in the midst of all the benefits of love, he cannot receive love itself and therefore loses the identity that was rightfully his.

Belovedness. Talk about stability! There is no spiritual groundedness in leadership without experiencing this truth at the center of your soul every day, without the active awareness of being loved lavishly and profoundly by God, at your best and at your worst. In this way, the principle of stability speaks directly to our greatest longing for affection and approval—and the outcome is living in our belovedness.

Feeling the Love in the Marketplace

Nearly all of what we have talked about so far relates most keenly to health in our souls; so what does this have to do with health in our leadership? Here's a little secret (maybe you've already figured this out): *The crux of being an effective leader is being an effective person.* Did you catch that? As Ruth Haley Barton puts it, "The best thing any of us have to bring to leadership is our own transforming selves."[4]

When your roots are deep and you are taking in great draughts of the love and life of God, you thrive—and then your leadership thrives. There are practical leadership skills to be honed for sure, but those skills only produce healthy leadership dynamics once you are already experiencing life as a healthy soul.

As we leave behind our compulsions to push the envelope by fanning the flame of urgency, and as we receive the gift of stability that comes from reveling in our belovedness, then effective leadership can emerge. Then spiritual authority is activated and imparted. Does that call to something deep in you?

Leadership stability is like the keel on a sailboat. A keel is a simple structure—a flat piece of wood or fiberglass on the bottom of the hull that plows through the water as the craft moves forward. To a novice, it might seem a bit superfluous, but it serves a crucial function—it keeps the boat from slipping sideways across the water instead of cutting cleanly through it. It provides stability plus direction.

And this is where unrooted leaders often fail, even Christian ones. A squall springs up, a crisis emerges, and people are panicking. Like in Jonah's story, the team, in a desperate bid to stay afloat, is throwing everything overboard that's not bolted down. Clear thinking and broad perspective are the first casualties when the stakes are this high and you're taking on water fast. The mettle of a leader will be displayed right here. If you can hear the whisper of the Spirit amid the thunder, then you're a person of stability. You have a keel. And this one quality can be the difference between sinking and sailing.

James, the half brother of Jesus, continues our nautical theme with this description:

> When you ask, you must believe and not doubt, because the one who doubts is like a wave of the sea, blown and tossed by the wind. That person should not expect to receive anything from the Lord. Such a person is double-minded and unstable in all they do.
>
> JAMES 1:6-8

No matter whether your leadership operates in the family room or in the boardroom, in serving communion or in serving the community, you need a keel. You and I need the principle of stability operating at full capacity. Benedict knew it then, and wise spiritual leaders know it now.

TAKEAWAYS

Here's a quick summary of the big ideas from this chapter:

- Stability touches the relational, geographic, and internal.
- Stability and urgency are mutually exclusive.
- The heart of stability is our identity as the beloved.
- Leadership thrives when leaders are anchored in love.

INTO THE MONASTERY

It's not enough to *understand* stability; we must *integrate* stability. We must *become stable*. We need to uncover what stability looks like in our particular settings, at our particular times. So before you step into the marketplace, I invite you to step into the monastery, as it were, to let God deepen this stabilizing force in your soul. Enter into a time of silence and solitude for God's formative work that takes place primarily in the heart, not the mind.

If you have access to a nearby retreat center or a place in nature where you can be alone with God, that is ideal. Otherwise, take this exercise into your daily quiet time or Sabbath reflection for some uninterrupted engagement with God and your own soul.

First, just take some time to let the torrent of compulsive thoughts taper off and grow still. Don't even pray in the sense we commonly associate with prayer: head-driven conversation with God. Instead, try something more like this:

- Read Psalm 131. It only has three verses. Gently mull over these simple thoughts and see if your soul will quiet down and be still.
- Ask yourself whether your recent leadership would be better described as a smooth-sailing boat or a wind-tossed wave. No judgment; just noticing.
- What is the invitation? What is the desire? Simply name them and hold them.

Consider what it means to be a stable leader, someone with a firm keel in the storm when others are blown sideways. Project that quality into any current crises or leadership challenges you're facing. Imagine yourself so rooted in God that the next approaching squall has you smiling in confidence instead of furrowed in anxious concentration.

Consider what actions you might be called to take to shore up a lack of stability in your soul. If this chapter has exposed an underdeveloped character quality in you, this is God's gentle nudge to put down deeper roots. Maybe God wants you to contribute to the stability of others. If that's true, what action do you need to take, and when will you take it? Put it on your calendar now.

IN COMMUNITY

Now, process this formation with your trusted relationships:

- Share the experience of your reflection exercise.
- Discuss the insights that appeared and the questions that were raised.
- Affirm the stability you see in one another now and in what's being formed.
- Pray for God's root care in your lives and your journey together.

A PRAYER FOR STABILITY

Join me in the following conversation with God:

Ever Stable One, hold me fast and close. Slow me down enough to lie quietly and peacefully with you. Keep me from always dashing endlessly forward, striving and performing to achieve and prove. Quiet my soul in your great silence and let me rest in your strong arms. Let me hear your voice, ever clear, telling me I'm your beloved, that you're pleased with me just because you are . . . and I am. You are you, and I am me. I am your child, and I'm learning to be like you. But that's not why you love me; you just love me. Let that truth become so fixed, so established within me that it's a keel of stability every moment of my life. Until that happens, just remind me every day of who you are and whose I am. Thank you, God. Amen.

3

CONVERSION

Not Fearing Scarcity but Trusting Abundance

We really must be quite clear that our prayer will be heard,
not because of the eloquence and length of all we have to say,
but because of the heartfelt repentance and openness of
our hearts to the Lord whom we approach.

RULE OF ST. BENEDICT, chapter 20

FRESH OUT OF COACH TRAINING in 2005, I was having lunch one day with a friend, describing my new career track. Halfway through my excited chatter about all the things I was learning, he leaned in and said thoughtfully, "Maybe I should hire you."

"Really?" I replied, shocked. Training was one thing; taking actual clients was another! But hey, this is what I had signed up for. I swallowed hard, summoned my courage, and said, "When do you want to start?"

Tim is the president of an IT staffing and consulting company in Greensboro—they hire out thousands of skilled computer programmers, financial managers, and other talent to large companies who need short-term project staff. Tim seems to have the Midas touch when it comes to building a business, but he was losing passion for his work, had toyed conflictedly with the idea of selling the company, and was carrying a lot of family stress into his workplace. He was far from thriving, and for the first time, he realized that he might have stumbled into some help.

Although this encounter happened many years ago, I still have a vivid recollection of sitting in Tim's corner office while he poured out his frustrations and confusion. The more he talked, the deeper he slumped over his desk, his body language eloquently mirroring his inner landscape.

As we explored Tim's leadership ambivalence over the following months, one thing became clear to me—and subsequently to him: God was uncovering character issues underlying his business concerns. In the years since, this has been a consistent thread in my work with leaders.

The pressures accumulating on Tim's shoulders were serving to provoke new depths of humility, a formational invitation not entirely welcome within his well-constructed facade of charming professionalism. The more we leaned into matters of the heart, the more clarity began to emerge for family dilemmas, as well as for his vision for the company. A year later, Tim no longer slumped over his desk; instead, he had a clear game plan and a lighter heart. Tim had stepped into the larger story.

Stepping into the Larger Story

It's easy to live painfully small lives. No matter what the title reads on your door or how many letters follow your name, life is often reduced to our modern version of *Survivor*: fighting through the weeds at work only to come home and negotiate a fragile peace with family members, pay some bills, be distracted ever so briefly by entertainment, and fall into bed to repeat the cycle the next day. *God, isn't there more to my story than this? Isn't there more beauty and more honor, something higher and nobler worth giving my energies to?*

Oh yes! There is a life of abundance yet. There is a bigger story that gives meaning to our small stories.

When we find ourselves here, as most of us have at some point, it's a wake-up call, a warning that we have fallen asleep to our true selves and our true calling, asleep to the expansive life of God that is shockingly abundant. Often it takes something more dramatic or traumatic to wake us: We've worked our way to an ulcer or an affair. A dream has imploded or a relationship has exploded. Maybe a loved one dies, and the pain jolts us from the stupor in which we've been walking and working.

Even our faith life can become small and dull, especially with the modern church's hyperfocus on justification. If "getting saved" is the high-water mark for ourselves and our world, we're still living in the small story, and our earthly lives remain eerily similar to those of our neighbors. What we often call *salvation* has been pared down to a mere nub of its true glory, as if the photo albums of our lives were limited to the days of our births. To be sure, day one was awesome, but it was just day one! Roughly thirty thousand will follow. Justification, priceless as it is, is just initiation into the life of faith.

When Jesus confounds Nicodemus with talk of a second birth, a spiritual rebirth into the life of God, he calls Nicodemus into a bigger story. He says that the end result of being born again is a life that can only be described as *eternal* (John 3:15), a term we have somehow attached to the afterlife rather than our current one. Fortunately, Jesus defines his terms for us during a final prayer before his earthly ministry concludes: "*Now this is eternal life*: that they know you, the only true God, and Jesus Christ, whom you have sent" (John 17:3, emphasis added). Rather than direct us to another point in time or another dimension, Jesus points to relationship with the divine—something unboundaried by either time or dimension. Eternal is both duration and depth. *"Eternal" is code for abundant*, and fortunately for us, abundance has no expiration date.

Take in some wise words from Parker Palmer:

> The quality of our active lives depends heavily on whether we assume a world of scarcity or a world of abundance. Do we inhabit a universe where the basic things that people need—from food and shelter to a sense of competence and of being loved—are ample in nature? Or is this a universe where such goods are in short supply, available only to those who have the power to beat everyone else to the store? The nature of our action will be heavily conditioned by the way we answer those bedrock questions. In a universe of scarcity, only people who know the arts of competing, even of making war, will be able to survive. But in a universe of abundance, acts of generosity and community become not only possible but fruitful as well.[1]

As we continue to unpack Jesus' prayer of abundance over his disciples, who will soon have to navigate their earthly journeys without his physical guidance, we see that his focus moves to several key themes, all of which apply uniquely to this world, though they are certainly not contained by it: *protection over their unity* (John 17:11), *an overflowing joy* (verse 13), and, in verse 15, an extremely earth-specific request: *"My prayer is not that you take them out of the world but that you protect them from the evil one."* Unity, joy, and protection from evil—now this hints of a larger story!

Jesus' prayers continue: *sanctify them* (John 17:17), *unify them* (again, in verses 21-23), and *instill the love of the Father in them* (verse 26). These prayers have the potential to lift our lives and our leadership out of the mire of drudgery and toward something approaching abundance. And as if that weren't enough, Jesus expands the unity theme even further: We will not only be one with each other (which we clearly struggle to accomplish) but will even be one with him (which feels so far removed from our western Christianity that it seems completely unapproachable).

It is our Eastern Orthodox brothers and sisters who have been much bolder to enter into this part of Jesus' prayer with their theology of *theosis*, or "divinization": *becoming united with God* (not to be confused with *becoming God*). The notable church fathers Athanasius and Irenaeus both wrote in support of this vision for our transformation into oneness with God. Surely this is the bigger story of our days! This journey to be formed into the image of Christ himself is the only story worthy of both Jesus' prayer and our great adventure. Only such a hope can elevate our existence beyond mere survival toward a life of courageous imagination. This Story is something the Benedictines called *conversion*.

Living False and Living True

For those of us who trust Benedict's guidance at this point, "conversion is not confined to a one time experience. To a monk or nun, conversion of life reminds them that everything they do is from, for, and with God and that God converts us continually."[2]

If this is an accurate view of the spiritual journey (it has revolutionized mine), then we have to learn the ways in which we obstruct (or fall asleep to) God's constant invitation toward conversion. The modern monk Thomas Merton (1915–1968) referred to this blockage as our *false selves*,[3] and I think the term serves us well. Every behavior that draws us away from God and away from love is patently false, an obscuring of the image of God within us. Or as Paul puts it, "We have this treasure [*what is true*] in earthen vessels [*what is false*]" (2 Corinthians 4:7, NASB).

Paul talks more directly about the false self with his constant reference to the "flesh" (*sarx* in the Greek), defined by scholars as "the earthly nature of [humans] apart from divine influence, and therefore prone to sin and opposed to God."[4] We are well familiar with our tendency to live "apart from divine influence," and Paul goes into some detail about it in Romans 8:4-8:

> [Those who live in their true selves] do not live according to the flesh but according to the Spirit.
>
> Those who live according to the [false self] have their minds set on what the flesh desires; but those who live in accordance with the Spirit have their minds set on what the Spirit desires. The mind governed by the flesh is death, but the mind governed by the Spirit is life and peace. The mind governed by the flesh is hostile to God; it does not submit to God's law, nor can it do so. Those who are in the realm of the flesh cannot please God.

Thus, our invitation into conversion.

The psychological word for the flesh or false self is *ego* (Latin for "I"). This is the self of appearances, the part we craft so diligently to look good and powerful and pleasing. It is not our true self and cannot be redeemed. So when we talk about conversion, we're not talking about reforming the false self; we're talking about the purposeful, grace-fueled movement away from what is false and toward what is true.

What we call *personality* is essentially, at least at the start, our personal falseness; as we mature, our personalities are meant to become more authentic, more true. If we return to the three fundamental human motivations from chapter 1—the pursuit of *control, affection, and security*—we can see how personality is our first instinctive move to claim those trophies in a world that feels increasingly out of control, hostile, and insecure as we grow up.

Some of our personality characteristics seem to be hardwired from birth while others seem to adapt to our environments, at least up to about age nine.[5] But whether they arrive at day one or years later, those personality preferences are utilized as strategies for meeting our core needs.

Some of us try to feel strong, lovable, and safe through extroversion—reaching proactively to engage others and shape our environments—while others try to accomplish the same goal by moving the opposite direction, attempting to fly under the radar and garner less attention through introversion. It's the same objective expressed in radically different strategies. The move to be a rule breaker or a rule follower, to be structured or spontaneous, to be a pleaser or a challenger—none of these are conscious choices, and none of them are inherently better or worse on a moral level. *What makes them false is that we think they work.* We think they will accomplish for us what we want most, and even when we notice that they don't, we keep doing them because we've found no other way of being in this world.

Until we are converted. Or, more accurately, until we begin a life of conversion.

The Paschal Mystery

I said a moment ago that we cannot reform the false self; there must be a movement away from the false and toward the true. But the reality is even stronger: The false self must not be merely replaced—it must die, which means that our life of conversion is a life of many, many deaths . . . followed by many, many resurrections.

Jesus explains this process using a simple metaphor: "Unless a kernel of wheat falls to the ground and dies, it remains only a single seed. But if it dies, it produces many seeds" (John 12:24). And then he goes on to illustrate this reality most powerfully in his own death and resurrection. But that's where we generally conclude the story—in the historical dying and rising of Jesus. So even when we recognize Christ's journey through death to new life, we usually miss the larger point that this is the life-death-resurrection process we are now called to replicate. Every day!

Paul picks up the conversation in Romans 6:4, saying that we died and were buried alongside Christ so we could be resurrected from death alongside Christ and "live a new life." Later in the same passage, Paul makes it clear that our virtual death and resurrection is an ongoing dynamic where we keep counting ourselves dead to sin so that we keep dethroning the reign of sin (verses 11-12). Within monastic communities, this ongoing experience of minideaths and miniresurrections is called *the Paschal Mystery*.

And while it certainly is a mystery, the deaths we undergo every day as we "crucify" the false self feel quite painful. It hurts to die. It's painful to let go of our emotional programs for happiness. Even though they have always failed us, we are attached to them. They feel like parts of us—and those parts now get to suffer and die! Many times over. But every time we take that courageous step and kill the false self by choosing the true, resurrection blooms anew. New life emerges with all the natal joy and wonder of a newborn child. We are not just born again; we are born again . . . and again . . . and again!

We're learning that conversion is a lot bigger and broader than we ever imagined. Let's keep going.

Awakening the Inner Observer

I love personality assessments. I'm fascinated with how the image of God shows up in such radically different forms in us humans. I've taken most of the popular ones out there and can now shore up my fragile identity by declaring that I am a CS on DiSC, an INFJ on Myers-Briggs, a 6 on the Enneagram, and Melancholic on the ancient Greek temperaments; and that's before we get to StrengthsFinder 2.0, the PDP ProScan, the EQ-i 2.0, spiritual-gift inventories, and the like. But until we use these powerful insights as leverage toward conversion, they're simply entertaining parlor games: fun but trivial.

For those of us who are married, we know that our spouses are both our greatest gifts and our greatest foils, the sources of our most enduring joy and sometimes our greatest pain. But one of the most powerful acts that your spouse will ever do for you— and hopefully will always do for you—is to hold up a mirror so you can see yourself as another soul sees you. This is the first step in awakening from the trance of moving instinct-driven and conversion-resistant through life, on personality autopilot.

I'll be honest: I don't always appreciate the mirror in the moment. It's usually a bit more truth than I want to deal with, particularly when I'm acting out in such a way that a mirror is called for. But one of the mirrors that my wife, Kellie, holds up for me periodically showcases my personality-fueled response to stress, which is most frequently triggered by my calendar.

Faster than you can say "double-booked," I will realize that all those tasks I have been so diligently arranging on iCal (in order to feel powerful, approved, and secure in my world) have crossed some invisible threshold and suddenly become overwhelming and impossible. *Danger, Will Robinson!* an inner voice screams in my ear. *You're going under, into the abyss of scheduling hell, where there will be weeping and gnashing of teeth.*

Seriously, in a matter of seconds, my stress level can go from imperceptible to redline. And my false self has a well-worn rut for responding to this scenario in very personality-appropriate terms. I fume and complain of the sheer injustice of it all—and Kellie is usually the one close enough to get caught in the toxic spew. She has found compassionate ways to let me know I'm entering false-self world.

If your stress response is different from mine, then you can see with hilarious clarity just how irrational and unproductive my personality response is, how it gets nowhere close to resolving the source of stress. Yet my default toward anxiety feels powerful to my ego, in a twisted way. Within that desperate feeling of powerlessness over a perceived lack of time, my "program for happiness" says that venting my frustration is a sure and trust-worthy way to feel happy again.

My program lies.

And so does your program. But we keep acting out those same self-defeating patterns of falseness with predictable regularity and equally predictable results . . . until conversion untangles the lie. But we can't untangle the lie that we can't see.

Usually we can only begin to see the lie once a spouse or brave friend holds up the mirror for us, which is a powerful start. But even that's not enough to initiate the conversion process. No, we can't rely on the observation of another; we must tap into our own *Inner Observer.*

The Inner Observer comes alive when we can distance our essence from our feelings just long enough to witness our emotions and behaviors from a place of objectivity, where we know that regardless of what we're feeling in the moment, *we are not our feelings*; where we know that what we "believe" to be true in a stressful moment is not entirely trustworthy and is more likely the result of our personality conditioning and habituated response patterns than objective reality; where we know that we do, in fact, have a choice.

By now you can probably see the connection between what I'm calling the Inner Observer and the role of the Holy Spirit, but I use this language to emphasize that this is part of our responsibility in partnering with the Holy Spirit. *We can cultivate this way of being with ourselves and with God by practicing the internal pause,* by stepping back from the intensity of whatever we're experiencing to observe ourselves, particularly in the light of our historical programs.

Here's the catch: The moment we observe ourselves being false—and start condemning ourselves for it—we throw a monkey wrench into the conversion process. Counterintuitively, beating ourselves up for what is wrong actually hinders God's work to draw us into the righteous life of truth. We have to train our souls to be gentle and nonjudgmental with ourselves, accepting the insight or correction in the light of our posture as God's beloved. And in view of God's abundance, we must embrace the shift from darkness to light with thanksgiving.

Your effectiveness as a leader of gravitas depends on the activation of your Inner Observer. Whether you're a small-groups pastor or a human resources officer or an executive director, you will carry little spiritual authority to develop others until you have fully engaged your own conversion. You can't observe *others* with clarity and compassion until you can observe *yourself* with clarity and compassion. The Jesuits used to say, *"Nemo dat quod non habet,"* which means, "No one gives what he does not have."[6]

The frequency with which we are oblivious to our own personality programs is staggering. Let's consider Paul's insight in 2 Corinthians 3:12-18:

> Since we have such a hope, we are very bold. We are not
> like Moses, who would put a veil over his face to prevent
> the Israelites from seeing the end of what was passing
> away. But their minds were made dull, for to this day the
> same veil remains when the old covenant is read. It has
> not been removed, because only in Christ is it taken away.
> Even to this day when Moses is read, a veil covers their
> hearts. But whenever anyone turns to the Lord, the veil
> is taken away. Now the Lord is the Spirit, and where the
> Spirit of the Lord is, there is freedom. And we all, who
> with unveiled faces contemplate the Lord's glory, are being
> transformed into his image with ever-increasing glory,
> which comes from the Lord, who is the Spirit.

We live in a world of veils, obscuring what is most true by holding up something more familiar, more comfortable. For the Jews, the veil was their "program of happiness" anchored in the Mosaic law, with its decrees and demands. Their performance within that system made them feel strong, lovable, and secure. But since that system was performance based, it fell far short of the gracious provision that Christ revealed. Our programs today are more subtle and personal, but they, too, hinge on our performance and so rob us of the gift that is grace.

As we cooperate with the Holy Spirit by activating the Inner Observer, we pull down the veil of what is false and step into the power of conversion toward what is true: God in us. God with us. God transforming us into the men and women he knows us to be—our true selves, our best selves no longer maladapting to the illusions of our inner world but allowing our minds to be transformed by the Spirit's power (Romans 12:2).

Our Resistance to Abundance

I was recently watching an interview with Brené Brown where she discussed how she had set few boundaries for relationships during the first thirty-five years of her life and how she had lived with resentment as a result. Eventually she discovered that she'd "rather be loving and generous and very straightforward with what's okay and what's not okay." This revelation revolved around her view of people: Previously, her honest assessment was that "people were sucking on purpose, just to piss me off."[7]

But one day she found herself wondering, *What if people are really just doing the best they can?* She concluded that whether that was objectively true or not (we never know), believing it to be true and responding out of that belief moved her toward the best version of herself. "To assume the best about people is almost an inherently selfish act," she admits, "because the life you change first is your own."

When we step into the world of abundance, it changes our lives with a pervasive conversion. I have experienced this time and time again.

Modern monk Richard Rohr observes that "our unhealthy economics and politics persist because even Christians largely operate out of a worldview of scarcity: there is not enough land, healthcare, water, money, and housing for all of us; and in America there are never enough guns to keep us safe."[8] Don't you find scarcity thinking everywhere? Businesses compete for a limited number of customers, potential employees compete for a limited number of positions, churches compete for a limited number of worshiping believers. This isn't spoken so much as simply understood, and behavior follows belief.

In a human world, there are certain limitations and constraints, so competition expresses a certain truth. But it's not the whole truth. And it's not the largest truth, even in this world. The divine world contains no limitations, and if we are to represent God's Kingdom accurately in our spheres of influence, we've got to tap into this alternate reality. Our mind-sets must be transformed so that we become part of the answer to Jesus' prayer, "Your kingdom come, your will be done, on earth as it is in heaven" (Matthew 6:10). To the extent that we operate in God's reality of abundance, we become agents of conversion, and the life we change first is our own.

I find there is something in me that, strangely enough, resists this truth. *How could that be?* Why would I ever choose to live with a mind-set of scarcity? A number of reasons, perhaps: social programming, personality angst, distrust of God in the face of past losses. Partly it may even be my own pathology to want to save myself by generating my own salvation. But see what you think about this: The reason we're tying a conversation on conversion to this theme of abundance is because *a life of conversion requires a God of abundance.*

Scarcity constricts while abundance enlarges. Scarcity breeds hoarding; abundance breeds generosity. If you see God's embrace as selective, God's people as remnant, or God's redemption as stingy, the life of conversion will elude you. And your leadership influence will reflect that constrictive, meager view of God by pushing people from behind instead of inspiring them by walking ahead. As a marketplace leader without abundance working in your soul, you will drive instead of lead. Without abundance, you will take instead of give. You will mandate instead of invite. But that's not the world we really want, is it?

Original Glory

Some of this thinking pervades our language around theology as well. The expression "original sin," found nowhere in the Bible, has been adopted across almost every denominational stripe. Although used to rightly convey our innate dependency on God's transforming grace, it carries a boatload of baggage in connotation. "Original sin" tends to bring with it a very low view of God's highest creation, rubbing our noses in a sewer of depravity and brokenness. Christian evangelists have polished that pitch to a high luster over the ages in their efforts to persuade men and women into the Kingdom.

Like the concept of marketplace competition in our earlier conversation, we find that a small truth stretched out of proportion becomes a caricature of itself and, at some point, becomes something that is no longer true. "Original sin" is a defective term, because sin was not original. Sin was not the original position of humanity. If something was original as it relates to the condition of human beings, then it must be glory. Right? We were created from a divine pattern to showcase the divine character. This is mind-boggling and paradigm-busting.

Eden demonstrates the original condition of men and women in right relationship to God—and we must be vigilant to hold this vision at the forefront of our theology, because this is what God is restoring. The glory of humanity is always a moon reflecting the glory of God, so we run no risk of a human glory that exists outside the divine glory.

Conversion is more than just playing nicely with each other; conversion is the move toward our place as sons and daughters of God. C. S. Lewis's well-loved quote is apropos here:

> It is a serious thing to live in a society of possible gods
> and goddesses, to remember that the dullest and most
> uninteresting person you can talk to may one day be a
> creature which, if you saw it now, you would be strongly
> tempted to worship.[9]

I know. It stretches my imagination to conceive of ourselves in such alignment with God and such transparency with God's glory. We're more familiar with Paul's lament in Romans 8:22-26:

We know that the whole creation has been groaning as in the pains of childbirth right up to the present time. Not only so, but we ourselves, who have the firstfruits of the Spirit, groan inwardly as we wait eagerly for our adoption to sonship, the redemption of our bodies. For in this hope we were saved. . . .

In the same way, the Spirit helps us in our weakness.

Some days we experience the groan; other days we experience the glory. But for modern-day monks, this thing is only headed in one direction: Conversion. Transformation. Redemption. And that is hope indeed.

In the next section of this book, we will explore more of the practices of conversion, for we are not passive onlookers in this drama. For now, we want simply to affirm our commitment to this journey and revel in the anticipation of God's work in and through us.

Carrying Abundance into the Marketplace

Agility has become a buzzword in the business world lately, and leaders' comfort with change and adaptation is an important skill in a marketplace changing as rapidly as ours. In fact, the connection between conversion and change management is a strong one. Markets move constantly, and the internal economy of an organization is also in constant motion as customers come and go, products are introduced and phased out, and windows of opportunity open and close.

The leader who adopts a welcoming attitude to the internal cycle of death and rebirth on a personal level becomes a leader who is comfortable with change, expects it, and expects to leverage change for positive outcomes on all sides. Leaders like this avoid the trap of attaching their identity to one business plan, one "rocket" product, or one sales strategy. Like my telecom CEO friend, they can discern trends with the full freedom to let go of what has been wildly successful once they see that it has run its course—like pay phones—and take hold of something new that is on the rise. This degree of agility in leadership is fueled by the internal life of conversion.

And now let's return to the personal side of the equation. Marketplace agility can be strategic, but *internal agility can be transformational.* And this is directly connected to our belief in and experience of God's infinite supply, both at work and at home. Leaders who embrace a lifestyle of inner conversion become spiritually agile, responding to the Spirit's illumination and renovation in ever-shortening time frames. The inner work that used to take years now takes months. What used to take months now takes days. It's not that efficiency is God's measuring stick for spiritual growth, but we don't want to hang out in that old, false self any longer than necessary, do we?

Agility, both on the inside and the outside, is a direct result of the life of conversion. Just ask the disciples. James, John, and Peter all dropped their nets and were converted on the spot from fishermen to fishers of men—that's an otherworldly agility, as is Saul's conversion from a persecutor of the faithful to their chief apologist. So we, too, unearth a newfound flexibility and response-ability as we embrace the humility of being converted daily.

Besides the ripple effect of your inner conversion on your outer leadership, there are other practical benefits. The more freedom you experience from your personality-driven programs, the more options you will see for responding to individual and organizational challenges. Rather than defaulting to familiar patterns that are either too conservative or too aggressive, you'll become open to new opportunities and new ways of thinking. That is priceless as a leader.

Freedom from your emotional programs will also make you more aware of how you have sabotaged relationships and marginalized teamwork in the past. The marketplace benefits of living in the abundance of conversion are myriad, but you can discover them for yourself.

TAKEAWAYS

Here's a quick summary of the big ideas from this chapter:

- The big Story of our lives is constant transformation (or conversion).
- Our personalities are often the face of our false selves that need more conversion.
- A life of conversion requires a God of abundance.
- "Original sin" often obscures God's restoration toward "original glory."
- Internal abundance leads to organizational agility.

INTO THE MONASTERY

I was visiting a thriving church in Pennsylvania and enjoying the deeply intimate worship time when the worship leader paused to offer a prayer. "We just can't thank you enough, Father, for how your sacrifice on the cross set us free. Your grace has liberated us. Thank you for saving us." His words were heartfelt and true—but they were entirely focused on a past event, what we in the evangelical tradition commonly call "getting saved."

This is not bad or wrong, but it is a truncated gospel. I expect that this worship leader and those who heard him know that sanctification is an ongoing work, but we need to expand our language around this concept to reflect the bigger story of ongoing conversion. What about a prayer like this: "We just can't thank you enough, Father, for how you continue to set us free— day by day, moment by moment, crisis by crisis. You lead us from death to life in daily transformation."

Worship is not just about looking back and thanking God for day one; it is also about gratefully receiving today's formational grace as we continue to experience the explosive power for change today and into the future. Grace has not yet completed its liberating mission!

In your "monastery retreat" or personal devotions this week, carry this broader perspective into your time with God using the three-phase conversation that follows.

- *Refresh.* Enter into the world of abundance that is God. As you sit in the stillness or walk a creekside path, take in the visual abundance that surrounds you. If you're not in nature, gaze at a piece of inspiring art. Listen to the abundance of birdsong or a moving praise song. Revel in the unboundedness of God's creativity and generosity. Let the truth of God's lavishness seep into the soil of your soul and inspire thanksgiving.

- *Reflect.* Think about your personality and what parts of it are most enduringly true—and which parts are merely props for your ego. How would you describe the false side of your personality, and how would you describe your God-breathed true side? What is God wanting to convert in you right now? How does God want to unveil his glory in your life more authentically in this season?

- *Refocus.* Now consider the quality of *agility* and what it means to engage in a life of constant conversion. What does God want to upgrade in your leadership now? As you think about the previous week of strategic-planning meetings and one-on-one training moments, confrontations, and celebrations, reflect on where you showed up in your false self. What would it look like to reengage those relationships and situations from the perspective of your true self next week?

IN COMMUNITY

Now process this formation with your trusted relationships:

- Share the results of your Refresh/Reflect/Refocus exercise.
- Discuss the insights that appeared and the questions that were raised.
- Affirm the conversion you see in one another now and where it's headed.
- Pray for God's root care in your lives and your journey together.

A PRAYER FOR CONVERSION

Join me in the following conversation with God:

> *Faithful God, you are determined to complete what you have begun in me, and I open my heart and soul to you this day in trusting confidence. I am amazed at what you have accomplished in me, yet I find myself daunted at times by the specter of all that remains dark inside. By your grace, I will not perpetuate false appearances through strength of personality; instead, I will humble myself before you and before others, acknowledging where I'm still in process and taking firm hold of your transforming power to make me like your Son, Jesus. I cast aside shame and celebrate your strength in my weakness. Amen.*

4

OBEDIENCE

Not Seizing the Moment but Surrendering the Control

Those who are possessed by a real desire to find their way . . .
live not to serve their own will . . . but they submit in their
way of life to the decisions and instructions of another.

RULE OF ST. BENEDICT, chapter 5

WHEN WE STARTED working together last year, Drew was wildly successful at everything he put his hands to; in fact, that's why he wanted coaching. As a pastor, he wanted some fresh help in organizing and managing the dozens of projects and ministry avenues that kept falling into his lap.

But despite all the overt success, Drew was also aware of something toxic just below the surface: his addiction to public attention, his compulsivity around validating himself, his spiritual shallowness. He held his life in a white-knuckled death grip. Somewhere deep inside, he knew that ninety-hour workweeks were unsustainable and perhaps even contrary to the gospel he loved.

After six months of three-steps-forward, two-steps-back, we sat down at an outdoor table at McAlister's Deli. It was a gorgeous spring afternoon with toasty sunshine holding off a chilly breeze while redbuds sported purple sleeves over awkward limbs. He opened with a telling statement: "I feel like I've stepped into a new pace of life, and it feels strange. I don't feel as productive, but I feel much healthier." Drew started to barrel on toward new goals to conquer until I stopped him.

"Did you hear what you just said? We've been working together for six months with the specific goal of hearing you say those exact words . . . and you're ready to fly by them. What if we just pause for a moment and savor what God has done with awe and gratitude?" And we did. Over a ridiculously large cup of lemonade, we celebrated the obedience of surrendering control.

Let's be clear. Drew's victory was not the result of better time management. And it wasn't even primarily the result of working through his priorities and behaviors. Underneath those important expressions of self-leadership, Drew was experiencing a different way of being. He was beginning to own a *belovedness* that defied performance and an *abundance* that punctured drivenness. He had opened enough of a window through his Inner Observer to move away from his favorite dysfunctional programs for happiness. And we were just getting started.

Who else benefits from Drew's stronger spiritual connection and more balanced work life? First up are his wife and three small children. You think they now experience more peace and love in their home as a result of Drew's realignment? I'm guessing they do. And their experience of God's glory through Drew as husband and father in turn ripples through their direct experience of God and all the other relationships in their lives.

And that's before we get to the thousands of people Drew preaches to and leads worship for and writes blogs for and trains as small-group leaders. The purposes of God expand exponentially in every small, secret act of surrender we embrace as we lay aside our broken programs and receive the supply of God as our overflowing source for all that our hearts desire most.

Leadership is never ultimately about talent or skill. At its core, it is always about character.

Another way of saying this is that leadership is incarnational. *We produce what we are becoming*, just as Jesus modeled for us. Jesus "took on flesh" (the literal meaning of incarnation) and "grew in wisdom and stature" (John 1:14, VOICE; Luke 2:52). He didn't just deliver the Good News; he *became* the Good News. His human life (the divine life notwithstanding) demonstrated what the Christian life is meant to be.

We will never be God (we don't need to, since that job is taken), but we are invited to incarnate the glory of God in our own lives. We are invited into the growing reality of oneness with God that Jesus declared: "I have given them the glory that you gave me, that they may be one as we are one—I in them and you in me" (John 17:22-23). That sounds like obedience to me.

The Profound Risk of Trust

For the Benedictines, I suspect that their application of obedience was channeled very tightly through the human leadership of the *abba*, the "father" of the community—first with St. Benedict himself and then with many other *abbas* as their communities multiplied. It was expected, no doubt, that the novices would yield unquestioning obedience to the direction of the *abba*. Yet it was ultimately with a Godward obedience in view, not purely a human one. The monks trusted the wise intent of their leaders and submitted to them as to God.

Only two possible motivations would lead men and women of
any era to give up the autonomy of their own wills and lay down
that power willingly: *fear* and *trust*. Both motivations understand
something essential: that we are either adrift in the world with
only our wits to secure us or, alternately, held in a grasp that is
both good-hearted and strong-handed. David had this same revelation in Psalm 62:11-12: "One thing God has spoken, two things
I have heard: 'Power belongs to you, God, and with you, Lord, is
unfailing love.'" God is both good-hearted and strong-handed. We
don't have to be afraid. We really can trust.

Fear sabotages all that trust by contracting both the internal
and the external. Fear is the language of scarcity; of cramped, com-
pressed living. All our attempts to "seize the moment" play off our
anxiety that we will lose the moment. Thus the native response of
the human heart is to grasp after control, an illusion at the best
of times. The result is disobedience, not to our spiritual leaders
perhaps, but to our own true selves—which is to say, abandoning
"Christ in [us], the hope of glory" (Colossians 1:27).

The rule of fear affects more than just us. Every time we allow
the spiritual dissonance of an internal or external disobedience,
we wound the world. Even though our Western understanding
of spirituality tends to be heavily privatized and individualized,
the reality is that we are much more connected than we know.
To pander to the false self is to wound ourselves. It is also—in
a mystical but very real way—to wound every facet of relationship with self, with others, with God, and even with the natural
world.

On the flip side, every choice we make to participate in the
divine life (obedience) is an act of healing on those same fronts:
self, others, God, and the world. So our obedience is of more

consequence than we realize. Even in the "small" choices. Even in the "secret" ones.

Obedience is not a popular contemporary topic. It feels so confining and old-fashioned, so uptight and Victorian and, well, monastic. It also feels vulnerable to the power agendas of others. Whether we're talking about obeying God or, worse, other humans, the whole topic is uncomfortable. So why would the Benedictines have made this, of all the many rich possibilities, one of their three fundamental commitments as a community? In a word: *freedom*. Obedience is the counterintuitive path to freedom and wholeness. We cannot be our true selves without it, and freedom is what we all long for.

Trust is the only container with enough flexibility and integrity to carry a life of obedience. And all our disobediences, from the most devastating to the apparently trivial, stem from a lack of trust. At each point where our souls draw back from joyful and immediate surrender to God's admonishments, we have succumbed to *the original deception of Eden*: that God isn't being truly good and loving toward us; that God is, in fact, holding out and is criminally disinterested in our happiness.

Happiness, Holiness, and Wholeness

I'm sure you've heard this little zinger from a TV preacher, delivered with moral conviction and unflinching certainty: "God doesn't want to make you happy. God wants to make you holy!" And maybe you simply absorbed it without question as the unvarnished truth. But this is a very dangerous misrepresentation of the Father heart of God that clothes a small truth in the bulky garments of a larger untruth.

Perhaps we can undress the deception by placing it in another context. Can you imagine making that same declaration to your adolescent children? *I have no interest in you being happy in my home. My only interest is in your obedience.* It would be absurd. It would be wrong. It would be cruel because we know, even in our all-too-faulty human parenting, that the very behaviors we are most eager for them to learn and respect will keep them within the boundaries of safety, well-being, and ultimately, happiness.

Pitting happiness and holiness against one another is an unfortunate dichotomy. True happiness, true holiness, and true wholeness are all part and parcel of the same great experience of being in alignment with God's character and wisdom for our lives. This foundation is essential to instill and constantly reinforce in the deepest places of our souls if we hope to have any paradigm for obedience as a core spiritual orientation for our lives. *We obey because we trust. And we trust because we know that we are loved beyond all reason and understanding!*

Perhaps this is a good place to revisit our overarching purpose in this book: to sink the roots of our spiritual lives down into the depths of intimacy with God in order to draw up the happy holiness of God, incarnate it in our true selves, and then live out of that gravitas in all our spheres of influence. Inspired by the monastics, we will reclaim a perspective and rhythm that can facilitate that very goal.

A Spiritual Revolution

The three Benedictine principles we're exploring in this first section of the book do not break crisply into clean, neat categories. Like most spiritual principles, they blur and blend into one another as part of the delicious, divine dance of God's universe.

But perhaps you can see that there is a certain sequencing of these big ideas . . .

The spiritual journey must begin with nothing other than *belovedness*. As that glorious truth begins to penetrate our psyches, we become able to live in a world as expansive and abundant as this love we have received. And as we experience the generosity of *abundance*, we realize that we can *trust* this great God of ours with everything: Nothing needs to be held back. Nothing needs to be protected and hedged by our emotional programs for happiness, not even our own freedom. No, *this great and beautiful God can be trusted with our greatest human offering: the unfettered surrender of unequivocal obedience.*

Speaking of our emotional programs for happiness, let's revisit those again as they relate to St. Benedict's three enduring principles:

- The belovedness that offers us stability also breaks our attachment to affection and approval. As we experience the expansiveness of God's affection and approval toward us, all our puny efforts to make ourselves lovable and worthy of approval become laughable—and unnecessary.

- The abundance that draws us toward conversion breaks our attachment to safety and security. Again, once we know how secure we are in the unlimited resources and care of God, we have no need to vainly shore up our own safety. All is provided.

- In this chapter, we're learning that the surrender of trusting obedience breaks our attachment to power and control. If God is in control and if God is trustworthy, then we can release our power agendas and fall into God's everlasting arms.

Not only does obedience require trust; it also requires humility. A willing surrender to God recognizes our desperate need for God. Like a two-year-old, we have such a small understanding of the world and ourselves, such a limited ability to assess reality and make healthy choices, that we need God's loving care and guidance on every level of life. Every day. All day.

The Invitation to Humility

I'll be honest about my personality struggles with obedience (I'm a 6 on the Enneagram, which we'll discuss more in chapter 6). I swing back and forth between two polarities: Either I can be too submissive, obeying without question and needing an external authority to validate myself, or I can be too rebellious, suspiciously casting off all external authorities in a desperate attempt at personal freedom.

But when I'm living in active awareness of my belovedness and God's abundance, with genuine trust, then I easily avoid those two pitfalls and hold my center, finding my inner authority in relationship with the Holy Spirit. From that place, I know when and how to submit myself to human authorities in God-honoring and self-honoring ways. When I fall short, it's usually a pride problem.

My personality doesn't lend itself to overt displays of pride. I am usually gentle and kind, rarely assertive or overbearing. My pride tends to stay well hidden, even from myself. It takes on the guise of responsibility: I will work hard, be organized and prepared, and not succumb to all the careless and unprofessional mistakes of those beneath me . . . I mean, *around me*. And yet despite my best intentions, I do make mistakes! And suddenly all the quiet judgment I have subtly bestowed on others comes crashing down on my own head with vicious self-incrimination. It is a tragic, violent cycle, one broken only by a simple quality of heart: humility.

I'm learning a lot about this these days. And when I say *learning*, I really mean having my butt kicked by it. Failing miserably, only to be rescued graciously. Time and again. No one said that spiritual formation comes easy. This putting down of spiritual roots isn't for sissies, no matter how much of a baby I am about it at times.

There's another whole reason to embrace humility, and that is because God is humble. I've known this for years, but it's still a stretch for me to comprehend—how the One who carries more power and authority than I will ever understand can also be the most yielded and vulnerable of all. It's a brain twister, but we have to wrestle this one down and come to terms with it on some level; otherwise we will never willingly yield ourselves in like fashion.

I'll offer a few examples: The Trinity's choice to elevate humanity into divine partnership as stewards of this planet was an act of humility (Genesis 1:28). Both the Incarnation and the Crucifixion represent the voluntary powerlessness of God in Christ. The radical humility of Jesus led to the radical obedience of Jesus. But perhaps the most dramatic and defining example of humility is the freedom God gives us to obey or disobey. *True love is humbling, not controlling.* It extends a costly and dangerous freedom—the freedom to say yes or no to the very love that guarantees its freedom. God humbly submits to our moment-by-moment choices about whether to surrender ourselves to the freedom of obedience or choose the captivity of our independence.

Attachment and Surrender

We've been talking a lot about surrender in this chapter, but what exactly is it? Surrender is the relinquishment of our own small wisdom in exchange for the all-encompassing wisdom of God. Like a "trust fall," surrender is letting go of everything that feels solid and safe, knowing that when we close our eyes and lean backward, we will be caught by strong, loving arms; passionately embraced; playfully tickled; gently caressed; and securely carried into Goodness itself. Why wouldn't we always do this?

Well, for starters, it's really, really scary. No matter how many times we have clipped into a zip line and ended the ride in laughing delight, there is always that initial plunge over the edge, the heart-lurching drop before we are caught and carried down the hill at excessive speeds that are both exhilarating and terrifying. We never get entirely comfortable with such vulnerability.

The other predominant reason why we resist surrender is that we're attached to something else. It's like clipping into the zip line without unclipping from the platform: You're not going anywhere! This is usually about attaching ourselves to our own version of the story as we believe it's supposed to be written. We attach to certain outcomes that we're convinced are good: the job we've wanted for so long, the SAT score that will get us into the perfect school, the one client who will meet our quotas for the year. Sometimes our attachments are pitifully small—catching the green light or not getting caught in the rain—and we sometimes even explode when these microattachments are thwarted!

Speaking of surrender, most real monks let go of all their money and possessions when they join an order like the Benedictines or Franciscans. This voluntary poverty is a dramatic way of detaching from their slavish service to the world's economic system, and it becomes a point of extreme freedom in choosing a life of uninhibited service to God and the community. It is a radical choice to dethrone "mammon" (Matthew 6:24, NKJV), with all its subtle controls and compulsions, and to yield completely in trust to the care of God. And while this feels like an unfathomable choice for most of us, the consistent testimony of the monastics is that this "sacrifice" brought them unimaginable liberty. Quite the paradox, isn't it?

Yet there remains a poverty of spirit that belongs to every one of us, and Jesus declared that blessing and happiness would attend those who accept it (Matthew 5:3). This poverty is attained in the daily, sometimes hourly, surrender of our preferred outcomes into the capable hands of God, so that God gets to determine what "good" looks like in our lives—which we'll recognize when we have eyes to see and hearts to receive the goodness that is given. This is the path of detachment and the path of freedom.

This all-encompassing surrender is challenged by the social contracts many of us pick up along our spiritual journeys. We easily adopt a subconscious belief that if we yield our lives to God as sincere Christ followers, then God assumes the obligation to take care of us . . . *in the ways we think God should*. Within this imagined "contract," there is very little wiggle room for potentially devastating circumstances: the implosion of a marriage, the early onset of Alzheimer's, the death of a child, a crippling accident, bankruptcy. Such tragedies either shake and fracture our faith in a good God or they bring us into the "fellowship of His sufferings" (Philippians 3:10, NASB) in all its raw and intimate vulnerability.

Only two things can transform the human soul: great love

and great suffering. The *great love* part is understandable—and desirable; it's the *great suffering* part that's not intuitive . . . and intimidating. There's something about loss and pain that has the potential to strip away our masks and defenses and open our hearts to change. This does not justify or explain evil; nor does it make God the author of evil. It does mean that good can triumph over evil (Romans 12:21).

Reconstructing Our Concept of Justice

The monk in the marketplace recognizes that God is both merciful and just (Matthew 23:23) . . . but these forces are not on opposite ends of the divine spectrum, as we have imagined.

In fundamentalist settings, it's easy to imagine God the Father as the holder of justice, angry and vengeful and compelled to punish disobedience . . . whose hand is only stayed by Jesus the merciful, who steps in front of us to take the bullet.

In this scenario, mercy triumphs over justice. One member of the divine community wins while another loses. This pits the members of the Trinity against one another and corrupts the entire concept of unity in community. But there is no divine wrestling match going on among the members of the Trinity; they are always in perfect alignment.

James testifies that "mercy triumphs over *judgment*" (2:13, emphasis added), not justice . . . and it's easy to confuse the two. Mercy can legitimately triumph over judgment because God's heart is not about judgment (1 Timothy 2:4); God is about justice, particularly for the poor and the weak, those who suffer the most from global injustices.

This isn't to say that there is no judgment in the world; there is plenty. Every sin, every turning away from the character and purposes of God brings judgment and death, as we described earlier in the chapter: We wound God, we wound ourselves, we wound others, and we wound the world. This is judgment, and we have "earned" those consequences—but that judgment is defeated by mercy in Christ.

The triune God does, in fact, experience anger. Scripture assures us that the "wrath" of God is a real thing (Ephesians 5:6), but we have to understand where that wrath is directed: toward sin, toward all the falseness, deception, and willfulness that hurt God's children (Romans 1:18), not toward the children. We don't hate our children when they disobey, but we hate what disobedience does to our children.

We're looking at the idea that justice and judgment are two very different things. Our misunderstanding comes from a skewed view of *justice as retributive*: that wrongdoing on one side demands an equal and opposite wrongdoing on the other side. Eye for eye. Tooth for tooth. Injury for injury. There were shades of this in the Mosaic law, and they served a purpose during the early years of God's people. But Christ raised the bar and forever refocused the direction of justice (Matthew 5:38-42).

God's justice in Christ is not delivered as *retribution* toward humanity but as *restoration* of humanity (Revelation 21:5). That is what divine justice is ultimately about. We humans aren't capable of this dimension of justice ourselves; we do what we can to rehabilitate offenders, but its effects are limited. Only God can lift us up out of our pigstys, just as the Prodigal Son experienced, and restore us into our destiny as true children of God. No punishment; just elevation.

In the Prodigal story, the father didn't go find another servant to beat because someone had to be punished for the Prodigal's wrongdoing. No, the father simply restored his penitent son to the joy, dignity, and fellowship he had lost. The son came home cringing and afraid, only to be amazed by what the disciple John so richly described in 1 John 4:18: "There is no fear in love. But perfect love drives out fear, because fear has to do with punishment." The mercy of God moves us past punishment to redemption.

Mystics and monastics have always known that we are not punished *for* our sins; we are punished *by* our sins. And that distinction is momentous. We don't die *for* our sins; we die *by* our sins or the sins of others. God made this clear to Adam and Eve from day one: "From the tree of the knowledge of good and evil you shall not eat, for in the day that you eat from it you will surely die" (Genesis 2:17, NASB). I figure that after their first tentative bite, the fact they remained standing seemed positive proof to them that somehow God had gotten it wrong. But death was blooming within their souls even before their lips tasted the forbidden fruit. It was in the turning from the face-to-face intimacy and trust, as William Paul Young describes so vividly in his novel *Eve*,[1] that the sting and punishment of death entered the human condition. But mercy and justice would team up to have the last redemptive word! And so they have.

What does this conversation about justice have to do with obedience? Everything—and it goes back to the divide between fear and trust. Who in their right mind would submit in obedience to an angry, vindictive God? If perfect love casts out fear, then it must cast out ours, if we would draw near in trusting obedience. This was the magnetism of Jesus, who turned the retributive undercurrent of the Old Testament on its head with a new definition of justice. For the woman hauled out of an adulterous liaison and threatened with retribution, Jesus dismantled that thinking decisively and restored her with a new revelation of God's idea of justice: "Neither do I condemn you. . . . Go now and leave your life of sin" (John 8:11). Mercy triumphed over judgment. Restoration triumphs over retribution. Now we can obey with perfect trust. What a relief.

The Human Factor

Have you noticed that we have yet to tackle one of the stickier applications of obedience—when and how to submit ourselves to human authorities? I mean, it's tough enough submitting to God, but at least we sort of want to do that, and we usually believe, at least theoretically, that God is trustworthy. But we know that people are often less than trustworthy. What then?

To simplify the dilemma, let me suggest that there are both voluntary and involuntary human authorities. There are many humans and institutions in our lives that demand a certain level of unavoidable obedience: Think of the IRS, the police, your high school teacher . . . these and many like them set boundaries around our behavior that we defy at our own peril. This level of obedience might have more to do with fear than trust.

God has something to say about such authorities. Paul reminds us in Romans 13:1 to "be subject to the governing authorities, for there is no authority except that which God has established." This doesn't mean that they are necessarily good or godly authorities but that we owe them a certain amount of respect and compliance, whether we trust them or not. And even Jesus calls us to "give back to Caesar what is Caesar's" (Matthew 22:21), a specific reference to paying our taxes and a general reference to living "at peace with everyone" (Romans 12:18).

Then there are the voluntary authorities that we choose (or at least accept) when we participate in a larger community or a desired experience—this would include your boss, your pastor or elder board, and your college professor. There is a certain amount of authority—limited to their spheres—that is accepted when you join yourself to a job or a church, and before doing so, you should establish whether that authority is credible and trustworthy.

An even more enduring context would be a marriage in which the husband and a wife are called to "submit to one another out of reverence for Christ" (Ephesians 5:21). In this passage, Paul connects the dots between our obedience to another flawed human being, a representative of divine authority, and our larger obedience to God.

Do any of these spiritual, vocational, or marital authorities have the right to abuse our trust or our bodies? They do not, despite their divine authorization. And because they are humans, this may occur, hopefully in innocence. Repeated abuses of trust challenge us to follow the biblical processes for relational confrontation, which will hopefully result in confession, repentance, and reconciliation that will heal the injury. When this happens, a powerful testimony is made to the restorative presence of God. Yet when all avenues for such reconciliation have been exhausted and when the stakes are high enough, it is right to remove ourselves from destructive voluntary authorities.

You may also experience destructive authority at work from another vantage point—as neither abuser nor abusee but as a third party who has both influence and opportunity to intervene and stop an abusive or unethical dynamic. Are you willing to put your own neck on the line to challenge an injustice when the stakes are high?

As we just touched on, all relationships—both human and divine—call us to an ongoing practice of confession and repentance in a spirit of humility and love. Because we are in a constant process of conversion, our obedience is continually won and lost. This is no cause for shame or dismay; it is our path. It is the life of hungering and thirsting for righteousness. Falling and rising again. Learning and transforming. Forgiving and being forgiven. We might as well get comfortable with confession and repentance, especially when we take our leadership into the marketplace.

Humble Surrender in the Marketplace

Remember, what we're reaching for as marketplace leaders is a depth of rootedness that can sustain our spiritual influence in the world. We're wanting to go deep more than wide. We want to carry wisdom that extends far beyond market savvy and carries actual authority. Spiritual gravitas allows us to release our vain attempts at controlling people and outcomes.

One of the hallmarks of spiritual authority is a wholesome blend of confidence with humility. As a monk in the marketplace, you can be bold because you act from a place of spiritual discernment rather than mere market principles, expediency, or manipulation. At the same time, the monk has no image to bolster or defend. Even the business guru Jim Collins describes the highest level of leadership as one marked by a profound personal humility.[2] And Patrick Lencioni similarly elevates humility as the quintessential trait of an "ideal team player."[3] These are astute observations from the marketplace.

We have discussed the utility of humility at length, so let's get practical. What does humility look like in the office day-to-day? Rick Warren describes it well, not as thinking less of yourself but *"thinking of yourself less."*[4] So there is a fundamental other-orientation at the heart of humility. There is an awareness that we are stewards of God in the divine Kingdom, not rulers of our own kingdoms—and as such, we are accountable to God for everything we do. Every attitude; every leadership meeting; every personnel decision, financial position, and strategic planning session are acts of stewarding God's resources, not ours. That's the vertical dimension of humility.

The horizontal dimension of humility informs every interaction with another human being: Every word, every facial expression, every motivation will either elevate others or elevate ourselves. *Elevating others is better.*

Humble leaders avoid being the focus of attention and redirect praise back to the team. They define success by how the entire organization (employees, clients, and customers) is benefited, not by how they are personally benefited. Without this quality of humility at the core of your leadership, you will inevitably leave relational damage and organizational debris in your wake. And your spiritual authority will be undermined.

TAKEAWAYS

The principle and the practice of obedience lead us to better understand our relationship with both divine and human authorities and to cultivate humility and trust as essential character traits. As a fundamental spiritual principle and commitment, obedience prepares us for a healthy relationship with the spiritual disciplines as a means of grace, not as performance.

Here's a quick summary of the big ideas from this chapter:

- Obedience flows out of either fear or trust. Trust is better.
- Happiness is the result of wholeness, which is the result of holiness.
- Obedience is the natural fruit of humility, and Jesus set the example.
- To surrender ourselves to God, we must let go of our attachments to outcomes.
- The justice of God is restorative, not retributive, which makes it safe to trust and obey.
- Human authorities are meant to be an extension of God's authority.

INTO THE MONASTERY

Each of these principles sets a high bar for our souls and our leadership. We know that even though we have come far, there is much further to go. None of us are as stable, as converted, or as obedient as we would wish, but rather than letting this be cause for shame or doubt, let it refocus us—with more clarity than we've ever had before—on God's destination for us. This is not about comparing ourselves to other people or to some ideal standard but about moving in the right direction.

Take time this week for some extended "monastery" time as you pray through this chapter's exhortations toward trust, humility, and obedience.

- *Refresh.* In this first phase of your quiet time, let all the preoccupations of your week simmer down from a roar to a whisper. Quiet your mind. Engage your senses. Often it's helpful to enter into some element of beauty—a forest path by a stream, a song that inspires your soul, a piece of artwork or poetry. Feel your soul shake off its crusty cloak of hiddenness, stretch, and step out into the sunshine. Experience afresh the amazing world you've been given: a world where you are infinitely beloved, abundantly resourced, and faithfully guided.

- *Reflect.* Consider your soul's condition as it relates to humility: What is there to celebrate with thanksgiving? What is there to confess with hope for transformation? What role does fear play in your life . . . and how willing are you to allow its continued presence? Invite God's transcendent love right into the center of your fear and watch it dissipate. Next, make an honest inventory of the things you are most attached to: Your career? Your reputation? Financial security? What outcomes do you find most difficult to surrender to the wise purposes of God?

- *Refocus.* If you're ready, actively release your attitudes and attempts to control each of these attachments; place them squarely in the hands of God, where all things are held with mercy and justice. Ask God where changes are needed in your life in order to obey him more completely. As you confess these places where you have missed the mark, receive God's abundant kindness and restorative power to bring the very spiritual alignments you are now requesting. Consider any practical shifts you want to make regarding your calendar, finances, or relationships as you prepare to reenter your life.

IN COMMUNITY

Now process this formation with your trusted relationships.

- Share the results of your Refresh/Reflect/Refocus exercise.
- Discuss the insights that appeared and the questions that were raised.
- Affirm the obedience you see in one another now and in what's being formed.
- Pray for God's root care in your lives and your journey together.

A PRAYER FOR OBEDIENCE

Join me in the following conversation with God:

Lord Jesus, Keeper and Restorer of my soul, I let go of my efforts to control or manipulate the people and circumstances in my world. In humility, I release all my desired outcomes into your keeping and trust you to direct my course far better than I ever could. Truly, you know what is worth preserving and how to preserve it. My great longing is to be obedient to your Lordship at every point, honoring you and others at every turn. Keep me attentive to your Spirit with faithfulness and joy as I return to my responsibilities today. Amen.

5

PRAYER

Not Taking Authority but Paying Attention

---

*God is present everywhere—present to the good and to the evil
as well, so that nothing anyone does escapes his notice; that is the
firm conviction of our faith. Let us be very sure, however, without
a moment's doubt that his presence to us is never so strong as
while we are celebrating the work of God in [prayer].*

RULE OF ST. BENEDICT, chapter 19

BOB IS A COLLEGE PROFESSOR in his late sixties who is accomplished and proficient in the business field. After ten years in the navy, he went on to higher education, where he has spent the last thirty-two years as a respected academian. Bob grew up in a home that, like all homes, carried its own dysfunctions. But unlike most families, both of his brothers suffered from mental disabilities. Bob persevered through the challenges of a family tendency toward mental illness to lead a successful career—externally at least. Internally he was plagued by frustrations and doubts that concerned him deeply.

Bob came to me for coaching, ostensibly for help managing, focusing, and organizing his life. Prayer and Scripture were already ingrained in his daily rhythm, and he daily asked God for guidance and empowerment to be a better leader, both inside and outside his classroom. Still, he floundered. Few besides his wife understood his inner struggle, but he confided in me transparently. Bob was possessed by a strong sense of calling, not so much for personal success as for national revitalization. He was clear that his role as an educator was meant to have exponential impact.

In our conversations, it quickly became apparent that Bob's struggle stemmed less from a lack of skill in planning and prioritization and more from a lack of spiritual rootedness. Driven by inner compulsions, Bob had difficulty experiencing the reality of being God's beloved, of living within divine abundance, and of surrendering himself to the trustworthy care of the Father.

As we began to explore his spiritual practices, Bob gradually but persistently learned the fine art of paying attention to his soul with all its covert motivations and habitual manipulations. Over time, he embraced the freedom of abandoning himself to the grace of God such that he began to integrate into actual practice the life-management principles he knew intellectually. Over the space of our first year together, the inner shift was remarkable.

The First Spiritual Practice

In most modern churches, there are simply two spiritual practices, and both are understood in very narrow fashion: prayer and Scripture reading. We are going to broaden those ideas considerably. For the Benedictines, there were a host of spiritual practices; of those many, they prioritized five, and these will be the focus of our next five chapters: prayer, study, work, hospitality, and renewal.[1]

Underneath every spiritual discipline lies one fundamental

discipline that we must incorporate. It is the first of the spiritual practices, holding the key to all other forms of spiritual engagement. It is radically simple, yet dangerously easy to lose in the daily scramble of life: the act of *paying attention.*

In the sleeper film *Cast Away*, Tom Hanks plays an up-and-coming FedEx executive. In an effort to whip a lackadaisical Russian distribution center into shape, he appeals to his professional motto: "We live or we die by the clock." He continues, "We never turn our back on it, and we never ever allow ourselves the *sin* of losing track of time."[2] Sounds familiar, doesn't it?

When it comes to paying attention, Hanks is consumed with getting packages quickly from point A to point B. His life is laser-focused on productivity and efficiency, and although these are legitimate goals, they don't leave much left over for a romance with his girlfriend. His frantic "gerbil wheel" career of running and globe-trotting comes to a crashing halt (spoiler alert) when his plane literally crashes in the Pacific. And though he miraculously survives, he spends the next four years of his life alone on a small island, where time takes on radically different significance.

The juxtaposition of Hanks's two lives is profound and invites us to reconsider our own relationships with time and attentiveness. Our attitudes about one will inevitably shape our attitudes about the other.

In the Western world, most of our lives are ruled by the clock from the moment we wake in the morning (at the behest of an alarm clock) until the time our heads hit the pillow at night (at the urging of that same clock). And almost every minute in between is allocated to tasks along a continuum of priority based on the hour hand and the minute hand.

The answer to this dilemma for some is the "5:00 a.m. Club." Feel like there's not enough day? Just create more day! Start the clock earlier—and perhaps push the clock later on the backside (*Sleep is for losers. The early bird gets the worm*, etc.)—and voilà, you've just stretched out a longer run time for the day. But here's the problem with that: Even if the "worm," the bait we're pursuing, includes spiritual stuff—even if it's *all* good stuff—success is still being measured by productivity. As long as that mind-set rules, prayer will remain a commodity, and the spiritual life will be bent to the agenda of accumulation. This is what happens when spirituality (and life itself) is subsumed by cultural capitalism.

For years, my daily sense of accomplishment—the one thing that most distinguished a "good day" from a "bad day"—was the sheer number of tasks I could cram into the hours between those two end points. It is a driven and relentless tyranny, but it also feeds our egos in ways that are enjoyable, ways we instinctively return to. Productivity tends to feed our sense of power, bring words of affirmation from others, and secure ourselves financially and emotionally. Remember those three?

In a world where time rules, even the best of activities, like spending time with God or making love to your spouse, easily slide into a box to be checked as you hurtle toward the next event. Our attentiveness in this mode gets laser-focused on two things: the task at hand plus the next one looming. We may "clock in" to work and "clock out" of work, but if we're honest, we're never really off the clock.

In such a culture, who has a chance to pay attention to anything besides project management? In this arena, there is little value or space given to pay attention to the bigger picture or to the more subtle shades of the spiritual world—which, of course, is why monastic communities emerged over time to radically reorient our attention toward what is most easily lost. As monks in the marketplace and cultivators of gravitas, we must reclaim the essential conviction that, as Socrates famously said, "the unexamined [inattentive] life is not worth living."[3]

A sixteenth-century Spanish monk named Ignatius (now known as Saint Ignatius of Loyola) used two words to help define ways of paying attention to the movements of God in our lives: *consolation* and *desolation*.[4] Consolations are those things that move us closer to God, closer to life, closer to love. Desolations are the opposite: those things that move us further from God, from life, and from love. Using these words in my own journey has immensely helped me to pay attention to the spiritual currents of my life, and I believe they will help you too.

Every spiritual practice—if it is truly spiritual—is a form of examining or paying attention to the movements of God, of the soul, and of the world around us. This takes time, but more importantly, it calls for a different mode of being—which leads us to the concept and practice of prayer.

Reinventing Our Idea of Prayer

In the second paragraph of Benedict's Rule of Life, he has this to say: "This, then, is the beginning of my advice: make prayer the first step in anything worthwhile that you attempt."[5] Seems clear enough, but let's dig into that. What does it really mean?

Most of us learned early in our spiritual pilgrimages that prayer is a conversation with God. Those from a more liturgical background ride the currents of ancient declarations crafted over time and collected into a book of prayer. Those from more contemporary worship communities emphasize spontaneous, heartfelt petitions. I have come to deeply value and practice both. But the overidentification of prayer with words invites various limitations and misconceptions. Let's explore a few.

Misconception #1: Prayer Is about Getting Answers

Some of the great catalysts for our prayers arise from a sense of need, difficulty, dissatisfaction, or confusion. We want to know what degree to pursue, which person to marry, or which business to buy, so we pray. We struggle with something that scares us or causes us pain—a physical ailment or lack of finances or an underperforming team member—and so we pray. We are frustrated with the direction of a relationship or our career or our church, and of course, we pray.

There is good biblical precedent for what are often called "petition" prayers, so this is legitimate. "Do not be anxious about anything," Paul instructs the Philippian church, "but in every situation, by prayer and petition, with thanksgiving, present your requests to God" (Philippians 4:6). Similarly, Peter urges us to "cast all [our] anxiety on him because he cares for [us]" (1 Peter 5:7). The Scriptures are replete with examples of God's people facing all sorts of crises and crying out to God in petition.

So what's wrong with praying for answers? Nothing, as long as we know whose answers we're really looking for. In most of our prayers, we are pretty certain we know the answers that are supposed to arrive—that the dying person be healed, that direction appear, that the pain be eased in whatever situations we are enduring. But if we petition God for the answers *we* want, we risk being disappointed at best or offended at worst. How many people have disgustedly thrown in the towel on their spiritual journeys because they didn't get the answers they wanted to an important prayer; because they didn't get the answers that they deserved and God owed them?

When the disciples asked Jesus to teach them how to pray, he chose words that reflected a radical trust in the answers God would give, in the extensive care God would provide—and they also came with an implicit yieldedness to the vast wisdom of God that often confounds my understanding: "*Your* kingdom come, *your* will be done, on earth as it is in heaven" (Matthew 6:10).

David Benner says that "when it comes right down to it, there are really only two possible prayers that can be prayed. One is entirely natural, one is absolutely supernatural. Whether we choose to pray or not, one of these will be praying itself. The choice is not whether to pray. The choice is which prayer to pray. The prayer that comes most naturally for all of us is, 'My name be hallowed, my kingdom come, my will be done.'"[6] This divide is the choice we face every day.

I dare say that every one of us has brought petitions before God on many occasions with all earnestness, asking God to do our will. The answer we want makes perfect sense. Surely God wants the same as us. We may even have chapter and verse to support it with certainty—and be wrong.

When we bring our genuine cares and concerns and needs before God in prayer, we want clarity about which of the two prayers is being prayed. *God only responds to one.* And honestly, we would only want God to respond to a perfect will, wouldn't we? Not a flawed will. Which is why God's deeper concern—deeper than us getting our way—is for our wills to "be transformed by the renewing of [our] mind" so we "will be able to test and approve what God's will is—his good, pleasing and perfect will" (Romans 12:2).

Misconception #2: Prayer Is about Taking Authority

Like the previous misconception, this one also has an element of truth in it. And it, too, happens to be easily prone to presumption and manipulation.

Jesus was not shy about referencing the authority he carried (Matthew 28:18). His authority was demonstrated in a constant flow of supernatural power (9:6-8) and repeatedly recognized by the awestruck crowds that followed him (7:28-29). Not only that; he also shared his authority with his disciples (10:1) while simultaneously cautioning them about how they carried it (20:25-28). Jesus well understood what human history has always confirmed: that power has a corrupting influence in human hands, even well-intentioned hands.

So in what sense *are* we to carry authority in prayer?

Maybe we can speak to an important nuance here by contrasting the words *carry* and *wield*—and looking at how they sometimes get expressed in the workplace. Perhaps you've run across an inexperienced leader who was put in a managerial position due to technical talent but who has no intuitive sense of how to lead a team. Sometimes, in moments of stress, such leaders will "wield" their authority, appealing to their positions in a clumsy attempt to bolster their decisions. It never works. Even when direct reports comply, that battle is already lost.

True authority is carried, not wielded. Whether supported by a formal position or not, real authority is felt and responded to without fanfare. This is the idea behind spiritual gravitas we've been discussing, and the same is true when it comes to prayer.

Christ in you carries authority, and we become the carriers of that authority when—and here's the all-important caveat—*when* we want, agree with, and pray for what is truly in the heart and mind and will of God. When we are in that place, we don't have to use the power words of *binding* and *loosing* and *declaring* to force God's hand. In fact, we may not even have to utter a single word, because we are already in the flow of his Kingdom coming and his will being done. Make sense?

There seems to be an endless stream of books on prayer that tend to sell well. And why not? Who wouldn't want to find the elusive key that allows us to "pray" our wills into the world? I don't question the motivation behind such efforts; surely they come from a desire to extend God's rule in the world. But just as surely, these methods tend to relocate the power for transformation into our hands in a way that inflates ego and minimizes the sovereignty of God. This is a danger worth avoiding.

Look at how Jesus avoided it. The Man with all authority, who could have summoned legions of angels to his righteous defense (Matthew 26:53), chose instead to release control, to shun manipulation, and to entrust himself entirely to a Perfect Will: "Not my will, but yours be done" (Luke 22:42). Should we do less?

Misconception #3: Prayer Is about Changing God's Mind

We have a few intriguing stories in the Old Testament that seem to show God wanting to do one thing, only to be persuaded to do another. One example is Abraham's negotiation with God over the destruction of Sodom and Gomorrah in Genesis 18. God is grieved over the cascading violence and immorality of these towns and confides his intent to bring their evil to a stop. Concerned about his nephew Lot and Lot's whole household, Abraham appeals to God: "Will you sweep away the righteous with the wicked?" Boldly, he gets God's agreement to withhold judgment if fifty righteous people can be found . . . and he proceeds to negotiate this number down to only ten. Unfortunately, ten cannot be found, and the cities are destroyed.

Many years later, Moses negotiates with God, more than once, over the fate of Israel as he attempts to guide them from Egypt's slavery into Canaan's promise. The Hebrew tribes complain, critique God's character, attack their leaders, and set up idols—all of which bring God and Moses into conversations where God threatens destruction and Moses intervenes. They all end the same way, as expressed in Exodus 32:14: "The LORD relented and did not bring on his people the disaster he had threatened."

These accounts of God "relenting" or changing his mind paint a picture that often finds its way into our modern prayer lives— the belief that if we pray long or hard enough or use the right words, then we can change God's mind that your mother's cancer will be healed; that your crucial deal will go through; that your prodigal son will return.

Here is the beauty of these ancient stories. *These epic conversations with God are not about changing God's mind but about changing the leader's mind!*

Moses is every bit as frustrated with his "congregation" as God. But when God calls on Moses to "leave [him] alone . . . that [he] may destroy them" (verse 10), he provokes Moses to lay aside his own frustration and lobby for mercy.

Where did that value of mercy triumphing over judgment come from? From God, of course! Did Moses come up with a more righteous plan than God's? When we look at it that way, the idea is absurd. No, mercy was God's intent the whole time, but this became a formational master class for Moses . . . as it must be for all of God's leaders. Including you.

I see an implicit four-step conversion taking place in Moses through his prayer conversations: identification (*We are your people; we belong to you*), compassion (*Remember us and forgive us*), intercession (*Lord, do not destroy; overlook our stubbornness*), and sacrifice (*But if you will not forgive them, then destroy me too!*) (Deuteronomy 9; Exodus 32). Oh yes, prayer is about change. But it's not about changing God; it's about changing us.

And so you can see how all three of these misconceptions *(Prayer is about getting answers, taking authority, and changing God's mind)* tie back to our original question: Whose will are we championing in prayer? I have tried to dismantle some prayer approaches that are most prone to sidetrack us from this precious gift of communion and partnership with God. Sometimes we have to dismantle what's broken before we can reconstruct a life of prayer capable of carrying true spiritual weight in life and leadership. If these are some things that are less true of prayer, what is more true of prayer?

The Posture of Prayer

In chapter 3, we talked about the endgame of conversion: coming into deep union with God. This result is incremental over a lifetime, of course, but it informs our understanding of prayer. If our earthly journeys are about being formed into Christ, then the "conversation" of prayer becomes more and more internalized than externalized. In other words, prayer becomes more a state of being than an activity, more communion than communication. If this sounds mystical, that's because it is. Mystical but very, very real.

Somebody somewhere came up with the clever observation,

"We don't know who discovered water, but we know it wasn't fish!" This always makes me chuckle, thinking about how water is all that fish know. It surrounds them, flows in and out of them, and makes up most of their bodies. Unless they happen to get lured onto a metal barb, water is their only and truest reality, but they can't see, feel, or taste it. It's too close to notice.

I imagine the presence of God as such a reality that so saturates our inner and outer worlds that it is all-encompassing. Sometimes it's too close to notice. But unlike fish, we can catch "glimpses" of it—*if we're paying attention*. If this metaphor is even close to the truth, then prayer really is as close as your breath and as constant as your heartbeat. And the invitation is simply to become more and more aware of what already exists.

With this understanding of prayer, we move away from compartmentalizing our lives: This is my work time, this is my family time, this is my prayer time. Instead, we move toward integration—all of life is work (or "worship," as the Hebrew translates it), all of life is family, all of life is prayer—and what we're really describing in the rhythm of our days is the brief refocusing of our attention on one or another. But they are all part of a whole.

I think this is what David was trying to grasp when he prayed, "Give me an undivided heart, that I may fear your name" (Psalm 86:11). *Heal all my fragmentations and unify my soul, that I may fear you.* "Fearing God" is the Old Testament equivalent to paying attention to God. God-fearing saints worshiped and obeyed God—but above all, they paid attention.

Here's another: "From everlasting to everlasting the LORD's love is with those who fear him" (Psalm 103:17). This is the way that verse landed in my heart this morning: *The more I turn my gaze toward God (pray), the more I experience the expansive love of God that holds me for eternity.*

So what we typically call "prayer" is a renewal of our attention on that part of our lives that is most deeply and pervasively real—which is why it's so powerful to weave these more active expressions of prayer through the fabric of our days.

David's profound revelation of this truth continues throughout his "journal." Reading these declarations, you can see how David maintained a more or less constant posture of attentiveness to God and to his own heart throughout his day:

- *"On my bed I remember you; I think of you through the watches of the night"* (Psalm 63:6)
- *"My mouth is filled with your praise, declaring your splendor all day long"* (Psalm 71:8)
- *"Seven times a day I praise you for your righteous laws"* (Psalm 119:164)
- *"Oh, how I love your law! I meditate on it all day long"* (Psalm 119:97)
- *"Have mercy on me, Lord, for I call to you all day long"* (Psalm 86:3)

Paul picks up the theme with his encouragements to pray "continually" (Colossians 1:9; 1 Thessalonians 1:2; 5:17), an image that only makes sense in this larger context of a way of being. Even the Benedictines didn't pray with words twenty-four seven; instead, an attitude or internal posture of prayer formed the container of their days, punctuated by eight specific times of focused prayer activity each day, once every three hours: lauds (3:00 a.m.), prime (6:00 a.m.), terce (9:00 a.m.), sext (noon), none (3:00 p.m.), vespers (6:00 p.m.), compline (9:00 p.m.), and vigils (midnight).[7]

That's an aggressive prayer schedule, and my own rhythm is decidedly less hardy. But the vision for remaining attentive to God in both waking and sleeping hours is compelling to me—not as a pressure, any more than fish experience water as a pressure, but just as a way of being.

Let's try to condense some of these broad perspectives into a handful of simple ideas.

Prayer Is Presence

One of the great challenges of life is finding the means to be fully present in each and every moment of it—every conversation, every activity, every person—and all the little fragments between them. Planning what we want to say while someone else is talking, attending to every beep and buzz of our smartphones, worrying over what's coming up—these are just a few of the ways in which we sacrifice presence in our lives. But what does that have to do with prayer?

Being present, being attentive, and having an undivided heart are all ways of describing the same dynamic. Until we can learn this way of being "all there" in life, it will remain difficult to be "all there" in prayer. But this is the great invitation of life: to be fully and consistently attuned to ourselves, to God, and to others. Simultaneously. Continually. This is prayer.

Brother Lawrence is a hero in many circles for championing this great truth, telling his simple story in the book *The Practice of the Presence of God.* Lawrence was a seventeenth-century French monk whose great occupation for forty years was washing dishes in the monastery kitchen. With remarkable joy, Lawrence transformed this humble service into an opportunity to cultivate awareness of the nearness of God, until life and prayer were fused into a single way of being. It's not the complexity of such prayer that eludes us; it's the simplicity.

None of this is meant to diminish the beauty and meaning of worded prayers. This more active expression of prayer is the natural overflow of a life of wordless attentiveness: a constant gaze, if you will, punctuated by utterances of affection and dismay, of deep longing and deep desolation, of the praises and petitions that comprise our days.

Prayer Is Alignment

Paying attention to these movements of God and soul ushers us into a surprising intimacy with the divine, and from that place, we begin to discern what is good and beautiful and true. In perceiving, we find desiring. Things begin to shift on the inside, as if we've been exposed to a powerful electromagnet. The intrinsic rightness (righteousness or holiness) of this Presence draws us toward alignment until something within begins to hum with transcendent resonance.

Prayer then becomes a point of access to our true selves, discovering who we are meant to be within this holy space of life. With equal intensity and gentleness, prayer exposes our false selves, highlighting those places of misalignment and brokenness. Prayer is never condemning or shaming but always invites us to return to Truth, always welcomes us into Love.

Prayer Is Surrender

The inevitable result of the journey of alignment is surrender. Rather than just yielding to God in part, surrender is yielding of the whole. It is the culmination of many microalignments along the way. But it is not a destination to be attained as much as an attitude to be embraced. The broadest surrender is the outworking of the deepest trust.

Hopefully you are already connecting these descriptions of prayer with the fundamental orientation of soul we unpacked in the first few chapters: Prayer is the unspoken voice of the beloved in response to Perfect Love. It is the conversation of the divine romance. It is our stability, our ground of being. Our rootedness.

Prayer is also the heart language of our ongoing conversion, the journal of our transformation into holy alignment, being "filled to the measure of all the fullness of God" (Ephesians 3:19). Prayer is both the means and the result of our realignment with God. It guides our discovery of and reveling in eternal abundance. It maps our practical access to these divine resources in the ups and downs of our days.

Finally, prayer is the glorious white flag of our surrender, the triumph of resurrection on the far side of death and defeat. A Belgian monk named Wilfrid Stinissen challenges us this way:

We have not surrendered our past with its guilt and painful wounds. We carry it with us like a heavy burden. Nor do we dare to surrender our future to God. We are afraid he will take advantage of our trust. How many there are who do not dare to pray: "Do with me as you will. . . . I thank you. I am ready for everything. I consent to all. May only your will be done with me and with all you have created!"[8]

Remember our emotional programs for happiness—the instinctive grab for *control, affection,* and *security*? Surrendering these needs to the care of Christ and receiving his abundant provision in all three categories lies at the heart of a posture of prayer. These are the moments when, as I quoted earlier, we're not living in the world for God, but God is living in us for the world. This is the life of trusting surrender. This is the life of prayer.

Monastery Meets Marketplace

Can you feel the inner tide change as we expand our view of prayer? Now let's bring these big ideas right into the practical center of the modern world. What would it look like to weave prayer into the very fabric of your daily leadership? Assuming you can't stop to pray for an hour eight times a day, where is the intersection between monastery and marketplace?

The answer begins as a new way of thinking—perceiving and experiencing prayer more as the "water" that we swim in all day long—and then moves to specific practices. Here are three very simple ways to integrate prayer more pervasively into your life and leadership.

Practice 1: The Welcome Prayer

Consider starting your day with this surrender of control, affection, and security—and an active welcoming of the Holy Spirit to guide and provide everything you need. Seat yourself comfortably in a quiet environment in an upright position, feet on the floor, hands loosely open on your lap. Close your eyes and relax your body. Quiet your mind, open your heart, and be fully present to this moment. Then pray the following:

Welcome, Holy Spirit.

I welcome everything that comes to me today because I know it's for my good. I welcome all thoughts, feelings, emotions, persons, situations, and conditions.

I let go of my agenda for affection and approval by receiving my belovedness. Welcome, Holy Spirit.

I let go of my agenda for safety and security by resting in your abundance. Welcome, Holy Spirit.

I let go of my agenda for power and control by surrendering to your grip on my life. Welcome, Holy Spirit.

I let go of my desire to change anyone or anything or even myself. I open myself to your presence and action within me today. Amen.

Practice 2: Praying the Hours

Sometimes called the Divine Office, praying the Hours is an easily accessible way to turn and return our attention to God as a daily rhythm. Simplified from the monastic tradition, there are four prayer points—morning, midday, evening, and night—and a host of ways to engage.

You might use these daily pauses for silence; you might use them to read Scripture or poetry; you might use them to bring timely concerns and celebrations before God in your own words. Historically, these four prayer points are times to join in reading and reflection of ancient prayers that for centuries have been lifted before God across the globe.

There are many sources for these crafted prayers—*liturgies*, for those of us from "low church" backgrounds. There is the *Book of Common Prayer* from the Episcopal Church, *The Divine Hours* by Phyllis Tickle, and other printed and online resources. Some are robust; others—the ones I use—are short and sweet, easily memorized yet profoundly memorable (see the resources list at the back of the book). You may find that these brief interludes anchor your day in God, renew your mind, and recalibrate your soul, sending you back into the next portion of your day refreshed and reconnected.

Practice 3: The Daily Examen

Another of Saint Ignatius's many contributions to the contemplative life is a practice he called the Daily Examen. This typically comes at the end of the day and can be done alone, with family, or with a work group. The Examen consists of quieting our minds and bodies and asking Jesus to guide us back through the experiences of the day, paying attention to consolations and desolations.

What moments were you drawn toward God and your true self? Which moments felt false and disheartening? What would God want to say to you through those experiences? What movements of presence, realignment, or fresh surrender arise as you prayerfully reflect on the journey of your day?

For Kellie and me, this is a time to pause at the end of work before starting dinner. With a glass of Chardonnay, we sit in our blue chairs in front of the fireplace or out on the deck when the weather is warm. Often we'll start with more of a practical catching up on the activities and experiences of each other's day and then shift into the Examen as we reflect and share the movements of God and soul. It's a beautiful way of keeping our hearts in the presence of God and sharing our lives with one another.

Remember that all three of these practices—and virtually every practice we encounter in the coming chapters—can be practiced both privately and communally. Keep that in mind, because you may need more of one or the other in this season of your journey.

TAKEAWAYS

Here's a quick summary of the big ideas from this chapter:

- The first and most fundamental spiritual practice is paying attention.
- Prayer is less about getting answers, taking authority, and changing God's mind.
- Prayer is more about presence, alignment, and surrender.

IN COMMUNITY

Within your small group, discuss your answers to the following questions:

1. How does prayer-as-paying-attention show up in your life right now? How would you express your desire to be more intentionally attentive to the movements of God and soul in this season?

2. How might these three specific prayer practices—the Welcome Prayer, the Hours, the Daily Examen— contribute to more stability, conversion, and obedience in your spiritual journey? If you could incorporate one immediately, which would you choose?

3. Where does your leadership need to be more present, more aligned, or more surrendered?

A PRAYER FOR PAYING ATTENTION

Join me in the following "worded" conversation with God:

Lord Jesus, thank you for continually teaching me how to pray. My heart thirsts for you, and my great desire is to drink deeply of you this day and every day. I want to incorporate my life in you into the practical flow of my work—never stepping outside of you but engaging with you while I write emails, talk on the phone, attend meetings, and make decisions—like taking constant sips from a spiritual water bottle. How I want your life to flow through me to everyone I touch today! Let your purposes be accomplished in all I say and do, but keep me mindful of you as I say and do, anchored and abiding. Amen.

6

STUDY

Not Tracking Trends but Fostering Wisdom

---

*You should take delight in listening to sacred reading
and in often turning generously to prayer.*

RULE OF ST. BENEDICT, chapter 4

BRUCE WAS A PROJECT MANAGER located pretty far up the food chain at a national financial management firm. He had a place of favor at his company, often getting to cherry-pick the teams he wanted to work with. But while he wasn't bored, he wasn't exactly inspired either. Frequently he found himself imagining what it would be like to use his talents for a venture that felt more altruistic, perhaps something in global-relief work.

Bruce hired me for some executive coaching, and we began to explore the source of his current dissatisfaction, as well as the hopes he had for making what felt like a more positive impact on the world. For months, we narrowed his focus of potential target organizations while he spruced up his résumé. Meanwhile, Bruce also enrolled in a course on spiritual formation, so that became a natural part of our conversations as well. As so often happens, we began to discuss the "bigger story" of his personal growth while we were working on the "smaller story" of a career change.

After about six months, I began noticing that Bruce's energy would surge as we discussed what he was studying and reading in his course, sharing transparently about the desolation of character flaws and the consolation of deeper spiritual practices. His enthusiasm was electric. At the same time, I noticed that the job search process felt more and more obligatory to him, more of an energy drainer than a motivator.

By *studying himself* and investing in his spiritual authority, Bruce was unconsciously developing wisdom and discernment. Eventually he realized that we no longer needed to coach around a job change; it was something that might come later, or not. Instead, he was finding ways to bring meaning and significance into his current world, and for then at least, it was enough. In fact, it was great.

Seeking a Heart of Wisdom

Good leaders *study their industry*. Really good leaders *study other leaders*. Great leaders *study themselves*.

After church a couple of weeks ago, I introduced myself to a visiting pastor and let him know that I enjoyed his message. In the course of conversation, it came out that I used to be a pastor but for an even longer time had functioned as an executive coach for Christian leaders.

Having done a bit of consulting himself, he asked a couple of thoughtful questions, starting with, "When a church has hired you for consulting, do you start with the pastor, the board, or the staff?"

"With the senior leader," I answered.

"And what topics do you engage first?" he continued.

I answered, "Helping the leader understand his or her own soul. Until a leader can discern their false self from their true self, they are untrustworthy and often do as much harm as good. Wisdom begins with self-leadership." This is what I have observed over the years.

The modern marketplace is not a forgiving place. The very economic engine that fuels the opportunities of free enterprise also leaves tire tracks across old enterprises that have lost their relevancy. Subtle shifts in materials, technology, pricing, and advertising quickly displace companies and even entire industries as newcomers push their way onto the playing field. The effect on leaders is often a long-term, low-level stress that becomes "normal"—a corporate PTSD, if you will.

The most common response to such abiding pressure is a frantic effort to stay abreast of all emerging data in any field that might affect their competitive edge. In real time. And the pressure that leaders feel gets inevitably pushed downstream until organizations are rife with anxiety, from top to bottom. It's not a pretty picture. More to the point, it breeds an environment toxic to the very quality that spiritual leaders most depend on: wisdom.

Leaders in the Bible—the good ones—were marked by a quest for wisdom. When it came time for Moses to engage his greatest enterprise, the Tabernacle, he would require a leader capable of overseeing thousands of workers who would be using innovative designs and materials. What qualities would such a leader need to have?

"See, I have chosen Bezalel son of Uri, the son of Hur, of the tribe of Judah, and I have filled him with the Spirit of God, with wisdom, with understanding, with knowledge and with all kinds of skills" (Exodus 31:2-3). *We run far too quickly after knowledge and skill to the neglect of wisdom and understanding, which come by filling and refilling ourselves with the Spirit of God.* Although few of us know the name Bezalel, I think we can safely say that he carried spiritual gravitas that showed itself, not just in the successful completion of a huge project but also in the larger purposes of God for his time.

And isn't that what we're really after—fulfilling the purposes God has uniquely given to us?

I love the way Paul describes King David's legacy: "When David had served God's purpose in his own generation, he fell asleep" (Acts 13:36). When we get to the end of our earthly journeys in life and leadership, I think that's pretty much what we want to hear said of us: that we grew into the character and accomplishments God had in mind for us.

Or as Paul also described, that we would follow in the footsteps of the early church leaders "to equip [God's] people for works of service, so that the body of Christ may be built up until we all reach unity in the faith and in the knowledge of the Son of God and become mature, attaining to the whole measure of the fullness of Christ" (Ephesians 4:12-13). I believe this is as much a mandate for Christian leaders in the marketplace as it is in the church. Have you seen yourself that way?

Wisdom does not come to us by accident, but by applying ourselves to what the Benedictines called *study.* "Studying what?" you might ask. Well, studying whatever might impart wisdom! This begins with the Scriptures but surely doesn't end there. Study includes reading the great spiritual writers, both old and new. Study includes gleaning from wise people in our lives. Study even includes transformational encounters with art and music as a source of revelation and worship.

Remember, though, that wisdom is not merely the accumulation of knowledge, no matter how worthy the knowledge may be.

Wisdom is about absorbing that knowledge into our being so that it becomes part of us. Wisdom is not the perception of truth but the incarnation of truth.

The Transforming Gift of Meditation

Last week I turned to my daily reading in Romans 14 and read some familiar verses. "Accept the one whose faith is weak, without quarreling over disputable matters," verse 1 begins. I read on through the paragraph as Paul offered a practical example and cautioned us against judging "someone else's servant," assuring us that it is "to their own master" that they "stand or fall . . . [and] the Lord is able to make them stand" (verse 4). I let my mind wash over this admonition and felt an inner "Yes!" rise in my heart.

What do you want to say to me about this, Lord? I asked. A face quickly rose in my mind's eye: someone I had a disagreement with. I began to see that person through a different lens, as someone whose faith is weak. But before that realization could translate into pride (*But of course I'm the strong one!*), I felt God's heart for this person. Kindness, compassion, and humility seeped into the raw places of my heart, and I began to intercede with genuine desire for peace and blessing.

But God wasn't done with me yet. *Are you quarreling over disputable matters?* I felt God's gentle nudge. I started to protest, *But these are important matters!*

The Holy Spirit continued, *And whose servant is this?* My protests died on my tongue. Rather than feeling ashamed (God never shames us), I began to feel a certain level of exhilaration. God can make that person stand! And God can even make me stand! Wow. What hope I felt, for both of us. Meditation had moved me into greater alignment with the heart of God and closer to my true self, the Christ-in-me self. It was that simple.

Fortunately for us, both biblical writers as well as the spiritual traditions of the monastics guide us to the process for incarnating truth: They call it meditation. Often viewed with suspicion because of its association with Eastern religions, the practice of meditation is anchored deeply in our faith. Consider a couple of the following examples.

The psalmist is the great champion of meditation. "Blessed is the one . . . whose delight is in the law of the LORD, and who meditates on his law day and night" (Psalm 1:1-2). The book of Psalms records at least sixteen instances where David and the bards of Israel speak about meditating on the words and the person of God.

The noteworthy leader Joshua was given this instruction by God: "Keep this Book of the Law always on your lips; meditate on it day and night, so that you may be careful to do everything written in it. Then you will be prosperous and successful" (Joshua 1:8). The truth is that Joshua had already established that very rhythm in his life, as we see in Exodus 33:11: "The LORD would speak to Moses face to face, as one speaks to a friend. Then Moses would return to the camp, but his young aide Joshua son of Nun did not leave the tent." Practicing the presence of God had already become a way of life for this young man.

Was the tent of meeting a place of prayer? A place of meditation? A place of divine encounter? Surely it was all of that. So the ancient tent of meeting—how does it show up in our world today? It shows up in us! Not in the housing of a church building, but in the housing of our very souls. "Do you not know that your bodies are temples of the Holy Spirit, who is in you, whom you have received from God?" Paul asks in 1 Corinthians 6:19. *The divine encounters of prayer and meditation now follow us, like a turtle carries its shell. We carry the tent of meeting with us.*

For the monastics, study and meditation were two ways of saying the same thing. It was only with the rise of the so-called Enlightenment in the eighteenth century that the Western world embraced a fierce rationalism that violently bifurcated the inner life between mind and soul. It has taken a very long time for this wound to be healed and the inner life to be unified once again— and again, it is the monks and mystics who have been used by the Great Physician for much of that healing.

My father is fond of describing meditation as "chewing the cud," an allusion to the way cows tend to make a series of meals out of a mouthful of food, visiting and revisiting it, tasting it over and over until it becomes part of their being.

It's not uncommon for Christians to approach the Bible much the way they approach a software manual: "If you click here and here, then enter your data there, you will get the following functionality." We search our online concordances for five promises that we can plug into our dilemma du jour, expecting instant solutions—and we're puzzled or maybe even offended when they don't work. This sort of flash-frozen spirituality is a recipe for disappointment, as is evident in the heartsickness of countless souls.

This is by design, because if God is committed to anything, it is to relationship. God will never allow spirituality to devolve into mere principles to be clinically manipulated for our own ends. The life of spiritual leadership will ever be one of face-to-face beholding, where rather than initiating the action, we are *acted upon. Meditation* is the biblical and historical word for this.

Meditation is ruminating, reflecting, and wrestling. Meditation is exploration, application, and integration. Meditation is conversation. Communion. Meditation is unavoidably personal. It is the path to revelation and transformation.

Looking in the Mirror

I mentioned in chapter 3 that one of the most powerful services a spouse can provide is holding up a mirror so the other spouse can see himself or herself. Perhaps as much as anything else, this is what professional coaches do in the marketplace: *They hold up a mirror* so their clients get a clearer picture of who they are, where they're going, how to get there, and who they are becoming as they move forward. To hold that mirror with both honesty and kindness, without intruding into the mirror ourselves, is a great gift to those we support.

Coaching is one powerful way to study yourself, but it's not the only way. Spiritual friendships are another way that we hold the mirror for one another, usually mutually, to promote growth toward wisdom. Whether in one-on-one friendships or in small groups where trust and transparency run deep, we can further the process of study in such a way that we are challenged by reading, conversation, and prayer to move past sticking points in character and behavior. In these safe settings, we can also be encouraged by those who believe in us, see us for who we are, and call us out into our best and truest selves.

In the fall of 2014, I was sitting in a bistro in Oak Ridge, North Carolina, across from a man I had come to trust deeply. Jeff had walked with me through many mountains and valleys of my personal and professional life, and that morning—over our usual breakfast of bacon, egg, and cheese paninis—he held up a mirror that rocked my world to its core.

I was at a low ebb in my business and was reaching hard to reinvent myself, trying to learn from the strategies of more seasoned coaches who had created systems that seemed to be working for them. As I complained and brainstormed with Jeff, a successful entrepreneur in his own right, he suddenly stopped and looked at me intently. "What?" I asked, sensing a weight in his presence.

He paused before speaking. "I just keep getting a picture that's kind of funny," he said, but his tone was serious. "I see a layer cake, and it's like you're trying to squeeze that layer cake into a Bundt pan . . . you know, the round one with the hole in the middle?"

"Yeah, I know," I replied, trying to understand where this metaphor was going.

He continued. "I keep feeling like you're trying to be something you're not." Now Jeff had my full attention. "I know you're trying to experiment with some ideas I've given you, but honestly, I don't think this direction is really authentic for you."

I was stunned. I had spent at least six months trying to ramp up a series of product offerings and marketing efforts with minimal success. And as usual, my approach when something wasn't working was to simply try harder. But the trying was taking a toll on my soul, and in a flash, Jeff saw it and gently but boldly called me out on it.

I sat in silence for some minutes while I digested this revelation. I was deeply invested emotionally in the track I was on, and I had no Plan B. While part of me knew instantly that Jeff was spot-on, another part of me resisted, feeling that to admit defeat was unacceptable. But my resistance crumbled quickly as pride gave way to relief: Maybe it didn't have to be so hard. Maybe I didn't have to follow the experts. Maybe my course was meant to be truer to me.

I quit that day. No one else knew except my wife and a couple of close friends. I continued to see clients and support those I was already working with, but on the inside, I had quit. I knew the path I was climbing was wrong, but I didn't know the path that was right, not for almost another year. Eventually I discerned the right path (largely due to a renewal in my spiritual practices), made the internal adjustments, and moved forward. But for about ten months, I had drifted, at a loss on where to go and how to get there. Perhaps you've learned how invaluable such humiliations can be; these times open us to our dependency on God like little else.

The practice of study isn't always this dramatic, but it is a formative force in the life of a marketplace monk. Pop sages like to call this dynamic "working *on* the business instead of working *in* the business," but in truth, it's more about being "worked on" than anything else. Human smarts simply aren't adequate to guide us in such waters. At crossroads like these, we can't even be coached into our course. We must be led. Good coaches know this and point us to The Coach for the deeper realignment we need most.

I am deeply grateful for the role that trustworthy friends have played in my journey, faithfully holding up a mirror when I've needed it. "The fear of the LORD is the beginning of wisdom," said King Solomon (Proverbs 9:10), and as we discussed in the last chapter, the word *fear* as used in the Old Testament has to do with where our attention lies. Study, then, is a natural complement to prayer as a way of attending to God's heart—whether we utilize Scripture, spiritual writings, song lyrics, or poetry; whether we study in solitude, with a confidante, or in community. At the end of the day, both prayer and study are about the core spiritual virtue of paying attention to what matters most.

Monastery Meets Marketplace

To grasp the benefits of study and bring them into our spheres of influence, we must break free from the "gerbil wheel" long enough to invest ourselves in a perennial thread of wisdom that runs through the ages, a thread of wisdom anchored in the Scriptures and extended by countless Godward souls since.

Practically speaking, this means retaining the childlike curiosity of a lifelong learner—and the practices that undergird it. So yes, study your industry. Learn what others are doing in your profession. As you are able, absorb the best technology and best practices of your field. But then go deeper. Those learnings alone will not contribute to your spiritual authority. Natural authority is given; spiritual authority is cultivated.

As you've seen, I offer three highly practical, easily accessible activities in most chapters, so you can experiment. The goal is not to do them all, necessarily, but to broaden your palette so you can choose where and how to deepen your roots. Some of these practices may be seasonal; others may become woven into the very fabric of your life. All of them have molded my spiritual journey deeply. And again, each one has both a personal and a communal element or application.

Practice 1: The Enneagram

I have spoken much in this chapter about the virtues of self-knowledge and self-leadership. Now I will offer you the best tool I know for doing that.

The Enneagram (pronounced "any-a-gram") is an ancient tool for understanding personality and behavior. Similar to popular assessments like MBTI and DiSC, the Enneagram offers insights into our most natural, basic way of being in the world—how we typically respond to relationships and environments. These insights then allow us to recognize when we are operating in the "low side" (false self) and help us choose the "high side" (true self) more and more often.

From the Greek for "nine" (*ennea*) and "points" (*grammos*), the Enneagram maps nine fundamental types of human psychology/spirituality and their relationships with the other types.[1] Going back to the fourth century, the earliest appearance of this tool is connected, appropriately, to a Christian monk named Evagrius Ponticus from Alexandria, Egypt. He identified nine "deadly thoughts" and the corresponding "remedies" that became the basis for the types. Several psychologists developed the paradigm further in the twentieth century to produce our modern version.[2]

I don't have the space here to develop the brilliance of this tool further, but there are many books and websites dedicated to its application in the modern marketplace, as well as coaches like myself who are trained to conduct the assessment. I highly recommend it.

Practice 2: Lectio Divina

Created by Saint Benedict in the sixth century and developed further by the Carthusian monk Guigo II in the twelfth century, the practice of "divine reading" is a way of approaching the Bible with a goal of *formation more than information*. The cool part of this is that the informational aspect comes automatically though more slowly, while the formational aspect becomes primary and intentional. Lectio Divina (pronounced "lexio diveena") is yet one more contribution of the monastic tradition that speaks powerfully to modern Christian leaders who desire greater rootedness.

Rather than simply reading a chapter of Scripture a day and then praying over our day, as many of us have been taught, Lectio invites us to engage God and our souls in a way that is immensely simple, efficient, and profound. It begins by taking a relatively short passage of Scripture, usually far less than a chapter—a paragraph or two is often ideal, a focused thought or story. Perhaps you will take these passages sequentially through a book or section of the Bible; perhaps you will take them from a lectionary schedule of reading. Either way, here are four steps to the Lectio process:

1. *Read.* Read through the passage once, slowly, thoughtfully, openheartedly. Let the words and the spirit of the passage wash over you. Be attentive to what word, phrase, or thought catches your attention. If nothing jumps out immediately, just close your eyes and let the passage rest inside you for a few minutes. Eventually something will rise to the surface.

2. *Reflect.* Read the passage a second time, holding that word or phrase before the Lord. What does God want to speak to you through this piece? What is God's invitation to you in your life right now? Where do these words challenge you, encourage you, or draw you toward the life of God, toward your true self?

3. *Respond.* Read the passage a third time. In this step, allow your heart to respond to God's invitation. This is your "yes" to the truth that the Holy Spirit offers you. There may be a specific action attached to your response, or it may simply be a matter of inner surrender to its claim on your life. You will know.

4. *Rest.* As you read the passage a final time, place yourself in this sacred space and rest. Remember, we talked about a cow chewing cud—ruminating, savoring, digesting, incarnating food into its being. That's what is happening as you read this passage over and over. It is an act of worship. The sentence or phrase you are drawn to becomes embedded. You will likely memorize it without even intending to. Throughout the day, your attention may be drawn back to this encounter.

Practice 3: Spiritual Direction

Another ancient practice from the monastic tradition is spiritual direction. Sometimes called spiritual "companioning," it is a combination of spiritual friendship, mentoring, and prayerful presence that brings a director and a directee into regular conversation over months or years together.

Commonly, these conversations fall on a monthly rhythm and are generally anchored in a question, concern, point of celebration, or need for discernment initiated by the directee. After this matter is expressed, there is usually a time of prayerful silence while both listen to what God is saying, leading, and doing through this matter. The expectation is that God will speak to both, not just the director, and both will share and discuss their perceptions of God's good intent. Here, too, there is a process of "reading" God's heart, reflecting, responding, and resting.

Occasionally spiritual direction may be integrated into a professional coaching relationship (I do this with my clients), but more commonly, this is a separate relationship from someone trained and focused in this specific way of "holding the mirror" for others on their spiritual journeys. I have worked with a spiritual director since about 2012, and it has been a game changer.

TAKEAWAYS

Here's a quick summary of the big ideas from this chapter:

- Good leaders study their industry. Really good leaders study other leaders. Great leaders study themselves.
- Wisdom is the ability to apply knowledge and skill under the direct guidance of the Holy Spirit.
- Meditation is the biblical and historical word for beholding God face-to-face, where we are transformed by his mutual gaze.
- Wisdom is not the perception of truth but the incarnation of truth.
- The gift of spiritual friendship is the ability to hold up a mirror to one another in courage and kindness.

IN COMMUNITY

Within your small group, discuss your answers to the following questions:

1. What are you learning right now from the process of "studying yourself"? How are you engaging that process practically?

2. How are you experiencing a meditative practice as a space for being "acted upon" by God?

3. Who do you most trust as a spiritual companion/friend/director in this season of your life, and how can you embrace that relationship more intentionally at this time?

A PRAYER FOR WISDOM

Join me in the following conversation with God:

Lord God, draw me ever deeper into the life of perpetual study and learning. Give me a childlike heart, a beginner's mind that is wide open to the transformational lessons that surround me with life-giving opportunity. Give me eyes to see, ears to listen, and an eagerness to respond to your many invitations to the True Self. Forge in me an enduring core of not just knowledge but wisdom. And let me become a source of Wisdom to all those in my sphere of influence. Amen.

7

WORK

Not Getting More Done but Being More Present

Idleness is the enemy of the soul. Therefore, all the community must be occupied at definite times in manual labor and at other times in lectio divina. . . . They will really be in the best monastic tradition if the community is supported by the work of its own hands.

RULE OF ST. BENEDICT, chapter 48

RICK WAS BORED. A rising investment professional at Wells Fargo Bank, he had survived constant industry turbulence as well as the absorption of Wachovia into Wells Fargo in 2008. It was no mystery to me why Rick kept landing on his feet: He was smart and personable, a compelling combination of IQ and EQ. But he was bored.

Ever seeking to expand his skill set, Rick wound up in one of my classes for training leadership coaches, where he was a natural. Restless, he flirted briefly with starting up his own coaching business, but somehow it didn't feel right. As I began to coach him on discerning God's path forward, one of Rick's values emerged and remained on center stage: his family. More than making a name for himself or satisfying his inner drive, he wanted to be there for his wife and growing family of five kids.

So rather than pushing, Rick put the brake on his itch for change and began to focus on being fully present to his family. With child number six on the way and his wife having decided to leave her job a few years earlier to give herself fully to being a mom, financial stability was critical. Rick wanted to take part in homeschooling and be available for ball games. That decision made it tough at the bank, but he remained committed.

In 2011, Rick joined forces with another bored bank executive, and they started making plans to launch their own wealth-management company. Five years later, Rick had engineered a merger with four other financial companies to form one firm with enough visibility and expertise to make a sizable impact in the city.

During this time, his spiritual practices flourished as he invested deeply in his personal prayer life and in ministry to other men. Alongside a few best friends, he continued putting effort into a small men's ministry they had started years earlier, focusing on strengthening their spiritual foundations and home lives. Rick became a study in "presence," showing up fully in every part of his world. The more he was transformed in that process, the more of a force for transformation he became with others.

In a growing firm, work productivity is a given; but I don't experience Rick as driven. Rather, there is a rootedness about him, a stability of soul that allows him to prioritize presence over productivity. You might call it gravitas.

An Invitation to Vocation

Contrary to monkish stereotypes, physical and intellectual work are core practices of the spiritual life. The Benedictines, along with virtually every monastic tradition, view work as a spiritual occupation. Although monasteries were often supported in part by wealthy patrons, Christian monks were rarely beggars. Instead, they supported the needs of their community by tilling the land, cultivating vineyards, and using their tradecraft for the benefit of all. Work was a holy thing, an act of worship (both "work" and "worship" come from the same Greek word, *latreuó*, and the same Hebrew word, *avodah*).[1] Even the most menial labor was engaged as a heartfelt sacrifice, an offering first to God and then to others. This experience is in short supply in the modern milieu, where work is often merely to be endured until a weekend reprieve.

Sometimes it seems that the contemporary workplace is reminiscent of the ancient tower of Babel. In a performance culture, size and influence are still what grab our attention. We are trying to build our own kingdoms, even in the name of God, that showcase the scope of our creativity and vision. Yet such kingdom building often obscures or even resists the purposes of God for the earth, and when it does, we find ourselves opposed by God.

The psalmist says that "unless the LORD builds the house, the builders labor in vain" (Psalm 127:1). How many leaders are building towers in vain today? How many of our business and ministry ventures have been more the result of ambition than the divine architecture that eases suffering and promotes health and community?

Maybe we've been building towers when God is more interested in a garden. Eden was the original human community and is perhaps still the best picture of God's original intent for the earth. Although access to that community was lost, the book of Revelation lets us peer into God's intent to restore people to another garden where "the river of the water of life" flows and "the leaves of the tree [of life] are for the healing of the nations" (Revelation 22:1-2). This is what we are made for, and this is what we are invited to co-construct with God.

Work as vocation brings a rich ethos to our understanding of the workplace and brings us into partnership with God's restorative vision for the earth. Every one of us is *called* to a type of work. Each of us has a unique gift that the world is desperate to receive and that usually finds expression in a job or career. Don't make the mistake of thinking that vocations and callings are limited to "the ministry."

We all know of jobs that feel like slavery, that seem to offer no reward to ourselves or to others. When we experience this, it is a clear indicator that we have yet to find or occupy our God-given vocations.

A few caveats here. First, most of us have to work our way through one or more jobs that are not our vocations before we enter one that is. Often, this is part of a discernment process for discovering our deeper callings, and sometimes it's a more pragmatic journey. Second, every job contains elements that are not necessarily joyful or satisfying; they just have to be done. Third, your vocation may exist more fully outside your workplace than expressed inside your workplace; that can be totally legitimate. But—and this is a big "but"—many leaders tragically fall into job ruts over decades, or a lifetime, that are tolerable at best and far from their divine design. Let's not be one of them.

Jim Collins is among the best business writers to perceive large-scale dynamics and communicate them in simple, powerful language that most of us can apply. He communicates truths that are true anywhere and everywhere, so what works in the marketplace pretty much works in the home, the church, and the public sector. I've never forgotten what he calls the "Hedgehog Concept"—the idea that *our sweet spot is found in the intersection among passion, skill, and profitability.*[2]

In other words, we all are passionate about some things—not just mildly interested or casually curious but gripped by the way things ought to be in the world yet are not. Sometimes coaches will ask questions like these to uncover passions: *If you could change one thing in the world, what would it be? What conditions or situations in the world make you angry? If you were independently wealthy and could do whatever you wanted, what would that be?* Another way of getting in touch with our true passions is to look back on our journeys: *When have you felt most alive, like you were most "in the zone," doing what you were really meant to do?*

Sometimes such questions provoke an emotional pushback: *Sure, I have lots of things that I'm passionate about, but this is the real world, and I don't have the luxury of chasing dreams. I have a family to provide for. Don't talk to me about passion!* I get that, and at times, that cynicism has crept into my own heart. But I hope you will allow me to say this: *There is a difference between chasing dreams and fulfilling a calling.*

I could get authentically excited about a number of vocations. At different times in my life, I have toyed with the idea of being anything from a fighter pilot to a medical doctor to a National Geographic photographer to an architect to a winemaker. Seriously, I can attach dates to each of those. Part of my personality is that I'm interested in lots of diverse things, and I could see any of the above as satisfying work.

But when I'm honest with myself, I have to admit that I don't really have the skill, the ability to excel in those fields. I can't be the best at those things, but I can be the best (or at least *my* best) in some things. And it's my job to find out what those things are and cross-reference them with my passions.

As Collins also points out, a passion-and-skill combo is an excellent starting point but not yet an ending point. If you have found something you care deeply about plus have a natural aptitude for, then you have found something precious. Don't ever dismiss or minimize it. But if it is going to be a career and not just a hobby, then it must be profitable at some level. There has to be enough demand for that product or service to "drive the economic engine" of your business and your family.

Some of us tend to be dreamers and chase visions that, however noble, aren't entirely functional in this world. Others tend to be pragmatists and seek career tracks that promise comfort, wealth, or prestige. Others are opportunists and simply take whatever presents itself when the time comes. My point is this: *Christian leaders who desire to extend God's redemptive vision in the world must be grounded in something beyond dreams, pragmatism, or natural opportunity. Our work must flow out of a confident sense of spiritual calling.*

The expression of that calling may shift over time, as it has for me: Vocationally, I have worked as a pastor, a writer, and an executive coach/trainer. But a single, unchanging calling fueled each of those different vocational expressions, one that began with a seed planted in my young heart at the age of thirteen. Figuring out how to live into that calling in a way that releases authenticity, practical provision, and seasonal alignment—that has been the quest of a lifetime.

And here's what Rick learned: The only way to rightly discern our callings is to be fully present and attentive in each moment of the journey. Attentive to God, attentive to our own hearts, attentive to natural opportunities, and attentive to those who know us best.

It's Always Being Now

Being present isn't just a means for finding and sustaining our callings; being present is essential for carrying genuine spiritual authority in the marketplace. There is a line in an old Van Morrison song that goes, "And it's always being now."[3] Just let that idea sink in for a few minutes . . . until your head explodes.

The only moment we have is this one. Right now.

And then this one.

We live in the now, or perhaps I should say that we are learning to live in the now.

Perhaps being present seems like a no-brainer to you. *Where else would I be?* might be your thought. But when we look at it more closely, it's not hard to see the many opportunities to get sucked out of the present moment. Consider these temptations:

- Invasive worries about financial stability
- Frustration over the revolving door on your executive team
- Strategic planning for the next quarter
- Lingering offense with a key vendor

As you can see, these are all common concerns in leadership, and each of them has some legitimate claim on our attention. It's not a matter of tossing such items aside; rather, it's a matter of recognizing what "now" is supposed to be about—and fully engaging in that.

The common element to each of these challenges is this: *They either pull you back in time to past events or push you forward into future events.* "Bad" is not the right word for these dynamics. Evaluation and reflection on past events are key ingredients to effective leadership, as is looking ahead to what is approaching from the future. The "bad" part happens when those *not now* dynamics displace the genuine needs of the *now*. Let's unpack that a little further.

The way to rightsize our past and future experiences as leaders is to bring them intentionally into the present. It is to ask the question, *What is the best response right now to my reflection on that past event?* Or *What is the best preparation right now for what we can perceive in the future?* That is living in the present.

Worry, regret, distraction, preoccupation—these are all symptoms of abandoning the present moment and losing ourselves in it. They are never productive; they cripple leaders every day.

One of the most common threats to presence is the ubiquitous myth of *multitasking*. Despite reams of research that dismantle the dated notion of multitasking as a leadership skill, leaders continue to champion this flawed idea. The complexity of the modern workplace is increasing—I'll grant you that. But multitasking is the very force that can sweep Christian leaders into the *mile-wide, inch-deep* syndrome and dissipate spiritual authority, not to mention efficiency.

No one can technically do more than one thing at a time. One thought at a time, one word at a time, one conscious act at a time. What we really mean by multitasking is the speed at which we can switch from one thing to another and the comfort level we have in that switching. To be sure, there is a vast spectrum of natural aptitude for switching. But every time we switch, there is a loss of energy, which means that there is an intrinsic inefficiency in switching—or there *can be*, when the rate of switching is raised to the level of "multitasking."

Whether you're "good at it" or not, *the first casualty of multi-*

tasking is presence. The ability to tune into the emotional atmosphere of a place or the subtleties of team interaction or the nudges of the Holy Spirit—all these evaporate when you get into multitasking mode. The leader with spiritual gravitas will seek to give himself or herself fully to one task or conversation at a time before changing gears, and as a result, they will carry more authority and, incidentally, get more done.

I must draw attention to one more giant thief of presence: *smartphones.* Several years ago, I was coaching a manager at an aeronautical-engineering firm, listening to him complain that he could not have a single conversation with his manager without his manager's eyes being stuck on his phone. Not one conversation. His boss would barely make eye contact with him because his phone was a steady stream of flashes and beeps. Guess how his direct report felt about that?

There is obviously a lot of competition for our attention these days, and life comes at us fast. This is true. But sometimes we have to push back! Sometimes we have to set boundaries for ourselves, walk against the hoard of lemmings crowding all around, texting their way off a cliff, so we can show up for the people in our lives. Whether it's your spouse or your client or your direct report, show them a little respect. *Go ahead; turn off the phone.*

Setting Time Management in Its Place

You have likely heard the perennial truism that goes something like this: *There is no right answer to a wrong question.* And one of the questions I hear a lot is, "What are the best tools for time management?"

Is time management a legitimate need? Of course. But in

most of my experience, when leaders ask this, they are trying to solve problems that cannot be solved by better meeting management, online calendars, and project-management software. Most of the time, the search for better time management is the wrong question.

If that's true, then it's fair to ask, *What is the right question?* Here's my take on that. The real question that most of us are asking without realizing it is, "Given my season in life, the condition of my soul, the resources available to me, and the work environment I'm operating in right now, what are my true priorities?" *Priority management, not time management, is the right quandary to solve.*

All leaders, if they're doing anything worth doing, have more good things to do in a day than can be humanly accomplished in a day. That is the world you live in. Wise choices about what to engage when is one factor separating good leaders from poor leaders. But if you are a Christian, you have one incredible conviction at your disposal—and you may not have even known it. Your deliverables, your responsibilities, and your task lists come not from a boss or a board or the stockholders. Not ultimately. No, they come from God. You are employed by God, and if your divine employer and your human employer are in disagreement, then you have bigger problems than time management.

The priceless conviction that you are employed by God leads to another equally priceless truth: God only expects a day's work in a day—not a day and a half's worth or two days' worth. If you really buy that, it takes an immense load off. Let's take this a step further. If you attempt to do one more task in your day than God is asking you to do, you are disobeying your Boss! And that's not going to play well for your soul, your people, or your company.

These core convictions are vital because they change the game entirely. Now, instead of trying to hijack new "time management" strategies to outsmart God and get everything done that *you* think you're supposed to accomplish in a day, your use of time becomes a matter of discernment. *God, what do* you *want me to work on today? And when am I supposed to stop for the day?*

Too Pollyannaish for you?

Well, give it a try. Spend thirty days asking God—in a serious way—to set your daily agenda; to tell you when to start, when to stop, and what to do. See what happens.

Monastery Meets Marketplace

I love the following lines from the *Book of Common Prayer*, a prayer of thanksgiving that expresses a healthy view of our work lives:

> *We thank you for setting us at tasks*
> *which demand our best efforts, and for leading us to*
> *accomplishments which satisfy and delight us.*
>
> *We thank you for those disappointments and failures*
> *that lead us to acknowledge our dependence on you alone.*[4]

Work is a gift, no doubt about it. Work was part of paradise, part of Adam and Eve's perfect world! I expect that the "new earth" (Revelation 21:1) will also have a way for us to engage our passions and talents (without concern for profitability) for the benefit of the heavenly community. Minus the thorns. Minus the curse. This is why work, even with its many thorns, is a spiritual practice for the Christian leader.

As usual, I'm going to suggest three exceedingly practical ways that you can harness the workplace dimension to be an extension of God's redemptive purposes in the world for his glory, your enjoyment, and the prosperity of others.

Practice 1: Discernment

To figure out what your calling is, or what God is placing on your to-do list, or how to set a Godward direction through your leadership, there is no substitute for hearing God's voice. Discerning that "gentle whisper" (1 Kings 19:12) is not a mysterious thing; it is a relational thing. When you invest yourself in paying attention to God's movements within and without by using the simple, ancient tools we have explored together, you will come to confidently discern his voice.

In that sense, discernment is not a practice per se as much as it is the result of a deep-rooted set of practices. But I will offer you some tips for leaning into this dynamic when you seek a specific answer to a specific question:

- Spend unhurried time articulating your question. This may seem self-evident, but often it isn't. Write down your question and then hold it prayerfully before the Lord. Ask him if it's the right question. Consider whether there might be a question behind the question that is closer to your heart's true desire.

- Hold your specific question within the larger context of what God is doing and saying in this general season of your life. Is there resonance or dissonance with the overall trajectory of God's work in you right now?

- Going back to Saint Ignatius's terms of *consolation* and *desolation*, consider whether your prospective direction takes you closer to God, life, and love or away from these things.

- Whom do you trust to give you wise, unbiased counsel in this matter? Which coach or spiritual director can help you connect the dots in the story God is writing in your life? If there is any biblical counsel on the matter, bring that into the mix.

- At this point in the process, make a tentative decision based on the discernment you have so far, and live with that decision for several days *as if you had already made it.* This is sort of a trial run. See if that prospective choice brings peace and confirmation or concern and uncertainty.

- Finally, look at your tentative decision in the light of our three core principles of stability, conversion, and obedience. How does your belovedness, God's abundance, and the freedom to surrender confirm or reorient your direction?

- Step boldly forward based on your discernment of God's leading. If God wants to adjust your path—and that may likely happen—God knows how to do it in ways that are gentle and good.

Practice 2: Culture Crafting

One of the most practical, impactful things we get to do as leaders is craft a culture. Managing your organizational culture is your first and greatest priority as a leader.

What is culture? I define organizational culture as the sum of values, styles, attitudes, and relational practices that govern a group of people. These are the intangibles that inform every conversation, motivate every task, and filter the environmental health of a company. And guess what? All of that is in your hands. In fact, if you've been leading your current team for more than a few months, the present culture is precisely the one you have created. Its strengths are probably your strengths and its dysfunctions are probably your dysfunctions. That thought is both sobering and exciting.

A myriad of tools are at your disposal for culture crafting, but realize that this is not a task you can delegate; this is an endeavor you must personally lead. Whether you draw on some great books or the partnership of a coach, culture management begins with you and will not go any further than you are willing to embody it. Here is one easy place to begin: assessment.

Use the simple questionnaire called *Culture Assessment*, located on my website at www.Thrive9Solutions.com/resources. Encourage your team to fill this out anonymously, compile the results, and then invite a strategic meeting to discuss your current reality, celebrate culture successes, and brainstorm strategies to improve your weak areas. The key to this exercise is total freedom of expression without defensiveness—just respectful, honest exchange.

Practice 3: Group Discernment

Remember Rick, the financial advisor who found his vocation? I had the privilege of serving on a nonprofit board with Rick for a couple of years. In this board environment, I got a chance to pilot a group-discernment process that I learned from Ruth Haley Barton.

Eloquently outlined in her book *Pursuing God's Will Together*,[5] Barton suggests a process for discerning God's will for your team and your organization, not just your individual life. Again, it's simple—and I like simple—but it is exceedingly rare to experience a team of spiritual leaders that work together in this fashion, even in the church. I commend it to you.

One caveat is in order here, and Ruth drives home the same point: Group discernment only works when the individual players are pursuing their own personal discernment and formation. This is a character-based contemplative practice, not a technique that can be commandeered.

Here is a simplified version of Ruth's group-discernment process:

1. Clarify the question for discernment.
2. Affirm guiding values and principles.
3. Pray for a surrendered heart, openness to God's leading.
4. Pray for wisdom and revelation.
5. Listen to one another.
6. Listen to God in silence.
7. Discuss perceptions and convergences.
8. Work with options and find agreement.

If you lead any kind of leadership team within a Christian context, you will find enormous benefit to working through this process and crafting a discernment culture using this resource.

TAKEAWAYS

Here's a quick summary of the big ideas from this chapter:

- Christian leaders who desire to extend God's redemptive vision in the world must be grounded in a confident sense of spiritual calling.

- Worry, regret, distraction, preoccupation—these are all symptoms of abandoning the present moment and losing ourselves in it.
- Priority management, not time management, is the right question to solve.
- You are employed by God, and God only expects a day's worth of work in a day.

IN COMMUNITY

Within your small group, discuss your answers to the following questions:

1. What adjustments to your work life do you sense your employer, God, requesting of you?

2. What does it mean to you to manage your priorities instead of your time?

3. What is your experience of living in the present moment— and of *not* living in it?

4. How would you articulate your vocational calling?

A PRAYER FOR PRESENCE

Join me in the following conversation with God:

Ever-working, ever-resting God, call me into fresh partnership with you today so that my work, however grand or menial, becomes a representation of your heart in this place. Where my vocation and my job are at odds, show me how to seek realignment. Where I am straining and striving to do your calling in my own strength, bring me back into harness with you. Where my work has ceased to be a joy, to myself and to those I lead, refuel me with your presence so that my leadership will be a source of life to everyone it touches. By the grace and mercies of Jesus, amen.

8

HOSPITALITY

Not a Tighter Focus but a Wider View

Guests should always be treated with respectful deference.
Those attending them both on arrival and departure should
show this by a bow of the head or even a full prostration
on the ground which will leave no doubt that it is indeed
Christ who is received and venerated in them.

RULE OF ST. BENEDICT, chapter 53

YOU MET JANET WARD BRIEFLY in the introduction; now I'd like to tell you more of her story.

Janet owns and leads a law firm dedicated to serving those who have been injured in various ways. It has been her intention from day one to make her company an extension of God's authority and care in the world, which she has done both in the immediate community her team serves as well as the global community, through going and giving.

About five years ago, God challenged Janet about going beyond personal tithes and offerings to tap the horsepower of her company. As a result, she has been giving away 10 percent of their revenues every year since, years lean and flush. Not only that, she has become a passionate advocate in encouraging other Christian-owned companies to do the same. Her world-sized heart is impacting such diverse areas as church planting, care for children, Bible translation, counseling centers, prison ministries, and a host of others.

Janet Ward has a gift of generosity, but in our work together, it has widened into a more holistic care for *all* those under her stewardship and leadership. The truth is, sometimes it's easier to give money to help others than it is to actually help others. And sometimes it's easier to care more for your customers and clients than your own "family." In fact, the bulk of my work as an executive coach is helping organizational leaders take better care of their own people and build a thriving culture. Janet Ward has exemplified that vision.

When I started working with this company four years ago, it was profitable, with a great reputation and a talented team. What it didn't have much of was internal unity. A rift between the "old guard" and the "new guard" was infecting morale. There was departmental siloing. There was a disconnect between attorneys and staff. Much good was being done for their clients, but the employees were not feeling the love, and a few were ready to bolt.

Bolstering her courage, Janet Ward waded into deep waters, asking hard questions. *Are we helping people work out of their strengths? Are people rewarded for instigating change? Is honest feedback welcome in our culture? How well do we communicate with our people? How is conflict handled? How are we at expressing appreciation?* Together, we began to look at the answers and plot a course for improvement.

Workshops, retreats, conflict resolution, personality assessments, coaching—all these were utilized to reveal what was present and to resource her forty employees with new mind-sets and tools. Of course, there is still work to be done, but the cultural landscape has changed immensely. Now, as much good is being done internally as externally. Now, the organization models the health and vitality that it is exporting around the city, the country, and the world. I love that.

Welcoming the Stranger

We tend to think of hospitality as either having guests in our home or that sector of American commerce that deals with hotels, conference centers, and the like. But in God's economy, we're all in the hospitality business.

I come from the evangelical church; this is my heritage. Prophets can only speak to "their people." It is only when you are part of a community, are fully vested in it and love it, that you can challenge it. So while I claim no official role as a prophet, I do find it unsettling when the most defining political and denominational distinctions of the church are nowhere to be found in the actual words of Jesus, while his most obvious, unequivocal statements are often ignored.[1]

Consider Jesus' clear declarations on nonviolence and the dangers of wealth, his bias toward the poor, and the upside-down economics of the Beatitudes.[2] When was the last time you heard sermons on Jesus' themes of downward mobility, surrendering control, and championing the powerless? It seems to me that the preponderance of today's sermons are clustered around the theme of *How do I use the teachings of the Bible to make life better for me?*

What would happen if we reevaluated our marketplace

leadership through the lens of serving the "least of these" rather than the most of these? Jesus used that expression to refer to the hungry, the homeless, the sick, and the imprisoned (Matthew 25:37-40). What possible connection could there be between your business or ministry and the "stranger" Jesus mentions in this passage? I think that's worth exploring.

The Choice for Space

Most business experts tout the virtue of focus in the marketplace, and for good reason. In our multidimensional, multitasking, multimarketed world, distraction and complexity are constant threats. We have addressed those enemies thoroughly in past chapters. Simplicity and focus are indeed assets for effective leadership. But if we stop there, we will miss a larger truth.

It is precisely because of our frantic, accelerating culture that we often stick our heads in the sand for sheer survival. Data overload is real, and a natural response is filtering out all nonessential information and opportunities—including the invitation to be a Good Samaritan. Including the chance to meet the needs of the least of these, at least the ones lying in our paths naked and bleeding.

There is a pragmatic message here and a spiritual one. The first relates to managing the tension between tactical leadership and strategic leadership. We have to know when to climb high in the tree, as it were, to see the big picture, and when to put our feet on the ground and deal with the needs of the moment. Great leaders learn how to juggle those competing demands with finesse. Living *in the now*, as we discussed in the last chapter, aids us at this point.

The spiritual message is similar: We must find a way to live and lead intentionally while maintaining enough margin to respond to the unexpected, to unscheduled opportunities for hospitality.

The Benedictines apply this in a very simple way: They welcome the stranger. They recently welcomed me to stay in one of their monasteries for four days. I prayed with them, slept with them (in my own room), and ate with them—at no cost! It was a remarkable experience that you can read about in my epilogue. But since you and I don't live in a monastery, how might we practice hospitality in the marketplace?

This capacity begins with "soul space," the ability to look around and see what's happening, to tune in to God's agenda when it interrupts ours. It reminds me of swimming in the ocean or a lake. To move with any speed, you have to put your head in the water and use the freestyle stroke, but when you can't follow the painted lines at the bottom of a pool, you have to keep popping your head up from the stroke to re-center on your destination and see what is going on around you. That gives you the chance to respond to an obstacle, a threat, or someone else in need.

For leaders in ministry or the marketplace, hospitality will remain a vague and inaccessible notion unless they cultivate a personal (and organizational) culture of attentiveness and margin. With the priority of hospitality and the practice of presence, we will be able to see the unique needs God is calling us to address.

Leading from the Poustinia

I'm going to hazard the guess that you've never heard the term *poustinia* (pu-steen-ia) before. It's a Russian word meaning "desert" that was used to describe a monastic role in the Russian Orthodox tradition. Once again, we uncover an ancient practice with remarkably relevant application to our current world.

Described thoroughly by social activist Catherine Doherty in her bestselling book *Poustinia: Christian Spirituality of the East for Western Man*,[3] the poustinia was a small, sparsely furnished cabin occupied by a *poustinik*. This monk devoted himself or herself to a beautiful blend of intercession and service. The cabin was located, crucially, on the very edge of the town—not in the thick of commerce and not out in the wilderness, but on the edge of the community.

From this location, there was enough silence and solitude to commune deeply with God and also enough availability to be reached easily by townspeople when they needed counsel, prayer, and encouragement. In addition, the poustinik would join the community when a practical need arose, such as harvest time or a threat to the village.

Doherty established several spiritual communities in Canada based on the poustinia model. They describe their ministry this way: "The poustinik is one who listens, and shares the love of Christ with all whom he encounters, as well as a cup of tea or some food; whatever he has he shares, as God has shared all with him."[4] Interestingly, her community in Ottawa calls itself a "poustinia in the marketplace."[5] Sound familiar?

So let's bring this home. Most of us are not called to a literal poustinia, but the ethos of the poustinia can inform our presence in the world. What does it mean for spiritual leaders in today's marketplace to lead from the poustinia? Or maybe better said, what does it mean to lead from the edge of the community?

This is a thoughtful question worthy of an answer. Maybe it contains a cluster of subquestions within it. Take a moment to jot down your thoughts on the following queries:

- *How can I live with one foot planted firmly in marketplace leadership and the other foot equally planted in the presence of God?*

- *How can I be fully available to God's agenda as well as to my people's needs?*

- *How can I stay focused on what I know I'm responsible for while still cultivating enough spaciousness and flexibility to be response-able to unscheduled needs and opportunities as they arise?*

These are right and necessary questions for leaders who want to carry God's heart amid the daily crush. Without these questions, we will simply be carried along by the current of our marketplace duties, well-intentioned but unrooted. We deepen our roots on the edge of the community.

The Economics of Abundance

Abundance has been one of our themes so far, and I have correlated it to the principle of conversion (chapter 3). We can't get to a flow of generosity without first being grounded in abundance. Makes sense, right? When we're constantly afraid of not having enough ourselves, there is little to no freedom to extend ourselves in hospitality to others. Follow this natural progression with me:

Abundance → *Gratitude* → *Generosity* → *Hospitality* → *Joy*

Growing awareness that we truly have all that we need (regardless of what the checkbook says) unlocks an unstoppable flow of gratitude in our lives. From that place of thanksgiving, we want to share our abundance with others in generosity. Once we get our eyes off ourselves, we can finally see and respond to the genuine needs of others through hospitality. And the result is inevitably joy. Happiness. Delight. Satisfaction and well-being.

So maybe we can "buy" happiness after all. Instead of by spending and consuming, it is through giving and serving that joy gushes up like a geyser. Unfailingly.

Jesus' values really spin us. He said, "Many who are first will be last, and the last first"; "Whoever finds their life will lose it, and whoever loses their life for my sake will find it"; and "I have come into this world, so that the blind will see and those who see will become blind" (Mark 10:31; Matthew 10:39; John 9:39). Jesus seems to be communicating that *his view of reality is completely opposite to our innate value system*, which means that if we are going to be the hands and feet of Jesus in the world, we must be reprogrammed at the very core.

Don't be naive at this point. When you start operating out of Jesus' economics in the marketplace, you will get pushback, just as he did. The interplay of values, social norms, and institutional rules that governs the marketplace is fiercely self-protective. When you work out of a different set of values, you will encounter dismissal, disdain, or even outright hostility, which is why Jesus calls us to "store up for [ourselves] treasures in heaven, where moths and vermin do not destroy, and where thieves do not break in and steal. For where [our] treasure is, there [our] heart[s] will be also" (Matthew 6:20-21).

As women and men of gravitas, we're trying to invest our hearts and our treasures in God's realm for God's purposes. Encouragingly, God's purposes have a good return on investment and contribute to bringing heaven into earth.

Monastery Meets Marketplace

We've explored some big ideas in this chapter: (1) the awareness that Jesus is more drawn to "the least of these" than "the most of these," and that if we intend to live and lead in sync with him, our attention should follow his; (2) the realization that it takes an intentional amount of time margin to respond to those in need; and (3) the poustinia as an image of merging compassionate availability with strategic withdrawal. Now let's look at some practical applications for cultivating a heart of hospitality in the spheres of monastery and marketplace.

Practice 1: Centering Prayer

This is an ancient form of Christian contemplation given modern form by Thomas Keating, an American Trappist monk who lived from 1923 to 2018. In contrast to most current understandings of prayer as an active conversation with God (praying with our understanding), silent prayer (praying with our spirit) accomplishes something different and complementary for the Christian leader (1 Corinthians 14:15).

Think of silent prayer as a form of hospitality; you are "hosting" the Holy Spirit. Practically speaking, it is a supersimple series of four movements:

- *Positioning.* Settle physically into a peaceful location free of distractions and make yourself physically comfortable. Choose a "sacred word" that feels meaningful in this season of your spiritual journey. (The word itself will not be the focus of your meditation but merely a tool for turning your attention to Presence.) Then set a timer for the desired amount of time. Perhaps start with ten minutes and increase gradually.

- *Noticing.* As you enter your time of prayer, you will soon become aware of a host of thoughts attempting to hijack your attention. This is not an enemy to be resisted as much as a habit to become aware of. Learn to notice your thought sequences with neither judgment nor attachment.

- *Returning.* Once you notice the thought that wants to dominate, your invitation is to release it and return your inner gaze to God's presence. This is where your sacred word comes into play: Brief inner repetition of this word gently leads you back into the present moment, just where you are—and where God is. You are not thinking *about* God but just being *with* God. This returning is the essence of Centering Prayer.

- *Confirming.* Once your prayer time is complete, take a moment to gently reawaken to the world. Invite a deeper breath, wiggle your fingers and toes, and softly give thanks for these minutes of *being* without *doing*. My personal favorite way to seal this practice and confirm God's activity is by saying the Lord's Prayer aloud. Then I move on.

Practice 2: Giving

Financial generosity is one of the great joys of the spiritual life. My invitation is this: Instead of giving to places or people out of expectation or habit, try asking God periodically where the Spirit might want you to invest. Be open to nontraditional giving; by that, I mean that the recipient doesn't have to be a 501(c)(3). While tax deductions are always welcome, the most Spirit-prompted need may be something else entirely.

Who is God bringing across your path, or what need is your path leading you to see? Stay alert for Good Samaritan opportunities and be willing to rearrange your schedule to respond to God's promptings.

Practice 3: Service

In the parable of the Good Samaritan (Luke 10:25-37), a man expressed his hospitality both financially and practically. As we said earlier, sometimes we can give financially but stay removed emotionally. But generosity is meant to affect both giver and receiver, and often this takes place most powerfully when it is our hands being used to bind up people's wounds and meet immediate needs, whether external or internal.

The concept of financial tithing (giving away 10 percent of our income) is well established in the evangelical culture, but what if financial generosity were matched by a generosity of time? What if we tithed our time, energy, and attention toward the least of these? That just might be a game changer, for you and for God's purposes in the world. All three of these practices—Centering Prayer, giving, and service—are expressions of spiritual authority released in the humble, unassuming spirit of Christ.

TAKEAWAYS

Here's a quick summary of the big ideas from this chapter:

- Welcoming the stranger is an essential part of spiritual leadership.
- Practicing "soul space" in our schedules empowers us to respond to those on our paths who are in need.
- The poustinia represents the intersection of action and contemplation for marketplace leaders.
- Abundance → Gratitude → Generosity → Hospitality → Joy

IN COMMUNITY

Within your small group, discuss your answers to the following questions:

1. What could welcoming the stranger look like in your world?

2. What do you need to stop doing so you are more available for unscheduled hospitality opportunities?

3. What is the vital message of the poustinia for you, and how can you respond to God's invitation in that?

4. What do you love most about generosity, and how do you like to express it?

A PRAYER FOR PERSPECTIVE

Join me in the following conversation with God:

Father to the orphan, Mother to the homeless, Healer of the broken, and Friend of sinners, draw us right now into your heart of compassion so that we might be as eager to follow as to lead, to serve as to be served, and to join the powerless as the powerful. Restrain our native self-preoccupation and empower us to see and care for others, even at our own expense. Revise our inflated view of leadership to that of servants and stewards to your children. And let us learn how to receive when we are in need; to not always have to be the strong ones. Thank you, Holy Spirit. Amen.

9

RENEWAL

Not Knowing Where to Go but Knowing When to Stop

When they have finished their meal they should rest in complete silence on their beds. If anyone wants to read at that time it should be done so quietly that it does not disturb anyone.

RULE OF ST. BENEDICT, chapter 48

I SERVED ON CINDY'S COUNSELING BOARD for about four years, until I moved to the mountains. You read my "stability" story with her back in chapter 2. During those years, we had numerous conversations about the challenges and benefits of taking a sabbatical. Cindy was a hard driver, pushing herself constantly—and constantly flirting with burnout. I wasn't the only one who urged her to consider taking some time off.

It took a few years for the seed to take root, but ever so gradually the idea of a sabbatical began to appeal to her. With her new board's support, Cindy decided to take one month away from the office—four weeks away from managing, away from clients and counselors and donors, to see if her tired soul could come back to life.

And oh, did it ever. She went on a backpacking trip in Idaho and tasted the sweet air of freedom.

When I spoke with Cindy weeks later, she was a new woman. She was back in the saddle, championing the healing of wounded souls again, but from a different place inside. I sensed a new stability in her, a new groundedness capable of withstanding the ardors of leadership. A greater spiritual authority. More joy. It was beautiful to behold.

Running on Empty

Not every Benedictine tradition includes this fifth core spiritual practice, but the wiser ones have come to embrace it. Why? The more naturally gifted the leader, the more he or she is "running on empty," working more and resting less, as Cindy did. My friend Fil Anderson wrote a book with that very title, sharing his story of doing Christian ministry without spiritual fuel.[1] When Fil and I first met, we compared notes and realized that we had walked a very similar dusty path.

The current is strong to seize every commercial opportunity yet ignore Jesus' invitation to "come with [him] . . . to a quiet place and get some rest" (Mark 6:31). Perhaps more than anything else, this threat will cripple the spiritual resourcefulness and authority of the modern monk, so this chapter will show you how to recharge your soul.

Even classic business thinkers like Jim Collins and Patrick Lencioni speak to the universal need to "sharpen the saw," Stephen Covey's term for renewal. Covey made the wise observation that you have to stop sawing—stop producing—in order to sharpen your effectiveness as a leader.[2] Why does it take so many leaders so long to learn this crucial lesson? I was thirty-four before I began to understand renewal, which was long enough. And I coach leaders in their sixties and seventies who have yet to grasp this vital truth.

How long will it take you? And what will be the cost—to you, your family, and those you lead?

One of the greatest enemies of rest and renewal is technology. I am not averse to technology, and I like upgrading my phone and laptop as much as anyone. But I have also learned a hard lesson: *that technology is not spiritually neutral*. Have you figured that out yet?

I used to think that technology was simply a benign tool that could be used for good or for ill, based on your character. Now, years later (typing on my MacBook Pro), I see it differently. Screens are drugs that lure us from more soul-nourishing engagements. Are they helpful tools? For sure. And I'm grateful for these tools. But if we are going to carry spiritual authority, we must learn that without vigilant boundaries, technology will dissipate our emotional and spiritual health. It erodes the soul, much like sugar erodes our bodies. So eat your cinnamon roll with cream-cheese frosting and stay current on your email, but understand that both are programmed to own you.

Technology, busyness, anxiety, drivenness, competitiveness, sleeplessness . . . these are just a few of the toxins in our modern world. Equipped with the spiritual practices of the monastics, your spiritual "immune system" will learn to neutralize those threats, keeping your soul healthy and your leadership trustworthy.

The Gift Nobody Wants

Interestingly, one of the first directives God gave to the nation of Israel was a disruptive one. To a primitive culture that depended on the daily planting, gathering, and herding of food—for their very survival—God said to take an enormous risk: Stop working one day out of every seven. *What?* Because few of us live in an agrarian world, we can hardly fathom the impact of this constraint.

But perhaps we can feel a bit of it once we try implementing it.

Modern Christian culture tends to view the Sabbath as a quaint relic of our Hebrew history. Or at best, a reminder to make sure we make it to church on the weekend. Who would possibly take the fourth commandment seriously today? In fact, I'm not sure how many modern believers know that Sabbath keeping is one of the Ten Commandments! Sure enough.

On the other hand, some Christians come from a more fundamentalist background, where Sabbath keeping was oppressive and joyless. Who wouldn't want to revolt from that view of God? The truth is that, like all of God's commands, the invitation to Sabbath offers a timeless gift to those with eyes to see and ears to hear. Ahad Ha'am famously said, "More than the Jewish people have kept the Sabbath, the Sabbath has kept the Jews." Somebody was paying attention.

The reason that Sabbath is one of God's greatest gifts is that it honors both work and rest. The implicit expectation of Sabbath is that six days will be marked by diligence, by using one's God-given talents to provide for family and improve society. Indolence is not a virtue; it flies in the face of the divine partnership God desires. But then, so does the workaholism that pervades our culture and is often cultivated, passively at least, by the church, with its many weekend demands. As I wrote in my first book, *Soul Space,*

At the root of Sabbath keeping lies a deep humility—the recognition and declaration that I cannot do it all, that I am not supposed to do it all, that God is God and I am not. Conversely, at the heart of frantic busyness and our subsequent soul clutter lies an incredible arrogance.[3]

"To act as if the world cannot get along without our work for one day in seven is a startling display of pride that denies the sufficiency of our generous Maker," declares Dorothy Bass. "When Sabbath comes," she explains, "commerce halts, feasts are served, and all God's children play."[4]

And as Mark Buchanan points out in one of my favorite books,

> Here's the logic of the Sabbath command in Deuteronomy: . . . Don't place yourself in a yoke that God broke and tossed off with his own hands. . . . If you loathed life under the threats and taunts and beatings of taskmasters, why reprise it? . . .
>
> The lie the taskmasters want you to swallow is that you cannot rest until your work's all done, and done better than you're currently doing it. But the truth is, the work's never done, and never done quite right.[5]

It is Paul who drives this point home: "It is for freedom that Christ has set us free. Stand firm, then, and do not let yourselves be burdened again by a yoke of slavery" (Galatians 5:1). Anyone ready to throw off those chains? We'll explore the practical opportunities in a little bit, but for now, I'll just leave you with a question or two: *Is freedom something you really want? How much do you want it?* The things that make for freedom are best woven into the tapestry of our lives as recurring rhythms.

Rhythm as the Heart of Leadership

When was the last time you paid attention to the cycles that surround our lives? Day and night. Waking and sleeping. Working and resting. Every aspect of our environment is ruled by a coming and going. *Rhythms and seasons are the essence of the created order and the backbone of our life journey.*

The orbital web of planets has a cadence, a drumbeat that regulates our seasons of the year, the phases of the moon, and the shifts of the tides. As I write this, I have only to look out my window at the ornate skeletons of bark and limbs that stand sentinel around my cabin on a chilly November morning. It's hard to believe they will all awaken from their coma in just a few months, risen from the dead, as it were. A grand tease, to be marked by hoots of laughter at the vernal punch line. *Gotcha. We were just sleeping—ha.*

So what if your leadership held the vibrancy of such rhythms? The ebb and flow of real work and real rest? Of outgo and inflow? Of praying the hours and managing projects, of spiritual direction and staff meetings, of Sabbath and spreadsheets?

Let's reach a little further. What are some of the other rhythms crucial to thriving leadership? Think about the continuum of noise and silence: Truly spiritual leaders know when to engage the thrill of purposeful energy and when to withdraw to the womb of solitude. They know when and how to speak, when and how to listen. They know when to do and when to simply be. Breathing in and breathing out: We can't do just one or the other; we need both.

If we feast every day, our bodies and souls groan with indulgence. If we fast every day, well, we die. The wise king Solomon once said, "There is a time for everything, and a season for every activity under the heavens" (Ecclesiastes 3:1). Rhythms. The flow and backflow of times and seasons are the fertility in which our gravitas grows and our roots go deep. In the next chapter, you'll have a chance to articulate the rhythms you sense God calling you to in this season of your life.

Monastery Meets Marketplace

The topic of renewal lends itself more to personal practice than to workplace practice, but I'll make a couple of points here. First, the more you embrace personal renewal, the more life and vitality you will bring into your workplace. You will bring a different kind of energy to your leadership. That's a no-brainer.

Second, as you increase your personal value for renewal, you will find that it shapes your organizational culture. Rather than believing good leadership means constant performance pressure on your team members, you will begin to want renewal for them too. The more you discover and integrate healthy rhythms in your life, the more you will set an example for them to follow. In this way, your personal practice will cascade into your workplace atmosphere. Let's look at a few specific practices.

Practice 1: Sabbath

We just discussed the reason for taking a weekly Sabbath, but what does that look like practically? We must resist the urge to create a one-size-fits-all approach to Sabbath keeping, which means that your direction for Sabbath must flow out of your relationship with

God. What might God be inviting you, personally, into during this week's Sabbath?

There are a few general principles, however, that can help guide us on the journey to rest. First, *don't work*. How do you know if it's work or not? I admit there are shades of gray here, but just be honest with yourself: If it feels like work, don't do it. Take a break.

Second, *accept the gifts of the day*. What brings you joy? Taking a nap? Going for a hike? Reading a book for pleasure? If mowing the yard is refreshing for you, then go mow. If having friends over for a wine tasting is fun, then invite away. If art delights your soul, then go visit a gallery. If doing nothing at all is what your body and mind need most, then by all means, do nothing.

Third, Sabbath is a day *to connect and to love*. Gather with your spiritual community. Have neighbors over for a drink or meal. Call a friend you haven't talked with in months. Snuggle in bed with your spouse. Visit someone who is sick or in need. Get creative. Follow your heart.

Practice 2: Personal Retreats

Periodic retreats have become part of the pulse of my days, the lifeblood of my leadership. Rarely a month goes by without at least an overnighter alone to quiet my soul and refill my divine-love tank. Have you noticed how you can fill the emotional tank of your children with intentional, loving eye contact? It's like magic. Wilted souls perk up with just minutes of such focused attention. We need the divine gaze in the same way.

The simple three-step exercise that follows reflects a rhythm I've fallen into for almost any extended time I take with God, whether it's an afternoon of prayer or a weekend spiritual retreat or a longer sabbatical. You have already used it in the first few chapters. I like that it's simple and flexible and can scale up or down to the time available. I like that it offers a gentle structure that keeps me from feeling lost in the space of the moment yet can adapt to the uniqueness of how I'm encountering God. I invite you to come into the monastery of your own choosing and either warm up to the inviting fire on the hearth or perhaps wander off across the open countryside. God envelops all.

- *Refresh.* Take some time to enter the world of belovedness. Let your imagination explore the dimensions of such unmerited favor. See yourself being baptized alongside Jesus and hear the Father's words spill over you, assuring you that you, too, are beloved and that in you, too, he is well pleased. Delighted. Dancing in exuberant, unquenchable celebration. Sheer joy.

   Let down your guard. Let go of your resistance, that part of you that wants to stop short and say, "But, but, I haven't . . . And I'm not . . . And I can't . . ." Allow yourself to be caught up in the bear hug of the Prodigal Dad. Both Henri Nouwen in his book *The Return of the Prodigal Son* and, more recently, Tim Keller in his book *The Prodigal God* point to the definition of *prodigal* as *not* meaning lost or morally corrupt; the root of the word is *lavish and extravagant*. That is the Father's heart toward you. Own it.

- *Reflect.* What is the message of your past or current season? Mentally scan over the recent weeks and months to connect the dots of revelation and understanding. The experiences you have perceived as either successes or failures—what are they speaking to you? What are you supposed to learn from them? Write it down.

Of the three emotional programs for happiness—*the need for control, the need for affection, and the need for security*—which one do you gravitate toward most often? How do all three typically show up for you? What tends to activate your sense of scarcity around those needs, and what do your "programs" look like? Journal your answers and talk to God about them. Write down God's perspective and how it differs from yours.

Now reflect on the abundance of God's provision for all three of those needs in your life—how God is powerful on your behalf, affectionate and approving without constraint, and committed to taking good care of you even in the midst of painful situations. Engage God in conversation and journaling on this topic too.

• *Refocus.* Consider the invitation to surrender yourself in obedience to God's trustworthy purposes. Name your desires for God and God's desires for you in this next season. What is God calling you to either emphasize or deemphasize in this coming time period? Who or what needs more of your attention, less of your attention? Write it down.

Here's a big question I have borrowed from Graham Cooke: *Who does God want to be for you in this next season of life and leadership?*[6] Hmm.

In this phase of your retreat, it's time to move toward the actions that will reflect your obedience to God. Make a list of the important tasks. Add and delete items on your calendar to better align with these new invitations. Now rest in the assurance that what God instigates, God empowers. You don't have to get the formula just right; you simply have to pay attention, show up, and engage the divine partnership. It won't all be perfect and pretty, but the journey will be good—definitely good.

Practice 3: Sabbatical

Sabbaticals are a natural extension of the Sabbath and were part of the communal experience of Israel. Every seven years (and every fifty years) the Israelites were called to step away from their normal responsibilities for an extended time of rest and renewal (Exodus 23:10-11; Leviticus 25:8-12). These extended Sabbaths were an even louder declaration of God's sufficiency and care to meet all their practical needs.

The essence of retreats and sabbaticals is solitude. Sabbaticals may not be entirely, or even mostly, alone, but the deepest work—in my experience—occurs in solitude. This is a practice embraced by virtually every monastic tradition, and I won't lie: Solitude is challenging. It tends to bring us face-to-face with our demons, the nagging questions and unresolved matters of soul that we can so effectively mask in the hustle and bustle of daily activity.

William Barry and Robert Doherty, as they chart the origins of the Jesuit monastic order, describe it this way:

> These Exercises put the [monastic] novice into the crucible of solitude where he is forced to face his alleged trust in God. He will confront his own self-will and sinfulness, his own fears and anxieties, his own weaknesses and strengths during days when he has few, if any, outlets that will divert him from this self-confrontation before God. . . . During these Exercises it is expected that the novice will experience various movements of the heart

that will agitate him and challenge him. He must learn to discern which of these movements are from God . . . and to put his trust in his discernment.[7]

Although this makes solitude sound daunting, these challenges occur within a safe environment: the unshakable love of God for you. In God's characteristic wisdom and patience, we are led precisely to what we are ready to see. We are inevitably led to places where God wants to liberate us from the false self and usher us into fresh freedom. I have personally come to find solitude the place where I feel most alive, most connected, most whole.

A sabbatical can be any meaningful length of time, but I recommend taking between three weeks and three months (sometimes longer) every seven years as a healthy rhythm of renewal. Before you scoff and discard such a suggestion as impractical or impossible, I would ask you to first honestly assess this question: *Would you if you could?* If your soul answers with a strong, authentic yes, then I guarantee you that a way can be found. Remember, we're not talking about a vacation per se; we're talking about a deeper kind of renewal. It will likely have elements of a vacation to it, but much more is going on here.

It's difficult to address all the logistics of sabbatical taking in this space, but fortunately, I have an extensive guide for this on my website. In fact, all the practices in this book are available for free download on my site at www.Thrive9Solutions.com.

Bonus Practice: Sleep

The medical community has begun to document the fact that sleep deprivation is now a national epidemic. While every physical body is wired a little differently, the target of at least eight hours of sleep a night is still the benchmark for optimal performance. Yet the national average dropped from 7.9 hours in 1942 to 6.8 hours in 2013.[8]

The point I'd like to make is that sleep is not merely a physical requirement; it also has a strong spiritual dimension. Aside from legitimate medical or aging challenges that some face, much of our physical mismanagement flows out of mismanagement of our emotional and spiritual dynamics—the very dynamics this book was written to augment. If this rings true, I urge you to reevaluate your prioritization of sleeping. There are also spiritual dimensions to both nutrition and exercise, but those lie outside the scope of this book. I leave it for you to explore them on your own.

TAKEAWAYS

Here's a quick summary of the big ideas from this chapter:

- We can only run on empty for so long before we begin to harm others and ourselves.
- Rest is a gift God is desperate to give us and we are often desperate to avoid.
- Rhythms and seasons are the heart of effective spiritual leadership.

IN COMMUNITY

Within your small group, discuss your answers to the following questions:

1. Just how weary am I in body, mind, and soul right now?

GRAVITAS

2. Historically, what has been my relationship with rest and renewal?

3. What "chapter title" would I put on my current season of life?

4. What rhythms need realignment in my life now?

A PRAYER FOR REFRESHMENT

Join me in the following conversation with God:

Lord, you see the weariness of my soul. I think I'm just coming to really see it—and to want something different. Or maybe I'm finally willing to move from wanting something different to doing something differently. I know that you are my source of rest—not just physical rest but also the deeper kind. Help me to embrace the humility, the obedience, and the delight of retuning the rhythms of my days to resonate with your best intentions for my health and calling. I don't want to be resistant to your blessings; instead, I turn my heart to receive them with gratitude. In Jesus' name, amen.

176

Conclusion

Rules, Rhythms, and Roots

---

*Any, then, who accept the name of [spiritual leader] should give
a lead to their disciples by two distinct methods of teaching—
by the example of the lives they lead (and that is the most
important way) and by the words they use in their teaching.*

RULE OF ST. BENEDICT, chapter 2

THE RESTORATION of Christian leadership is as simple as it is timeless: reclaiming the principles and practices of the ancients in the context of a modern world. This is not for the sequestered few but for today's entrepreneurs and pastors and executives and business owners—for everyone who wants to be spiritually significant in ways small and large.

In the introduction, I used the metaphor of a tree—the larger the reach of our branches, the greater must be the depth of our roots. It's not about becoming a spiritual big shot; it's about being who we are meant to be. "Christ is in you, so therefore you can look forward to sharing in God's glory," Paul describes it (Colossians 1:27, MSG). If anything glorious is going to come out of our lives, it's going to come from the Spirit of God within us.

This book is simply about making room for the Spirit's manifestation in and through us, not to draw attention to ourselves but to draw attention to the beauty and goodness of God.

We have covered a lot of ground by looking at how an ancient spiritual community called the Benedictines simplified their focus to three core principles—stability, conversion, and obedience—and then oriented their practical lives around five core practices—prayer, study, work, hospitality, and renewal. Unless you really are a monk living in a monastery, this will not be the sum of your life. Instead, our lives in the marketplace can be infused with and grounded in our lives in God in ways that reflect the wisdom of the monastery.

If you're like me, the call to gravitas is both captivating and overwhelming. In this final chapter, we're going to take away the overwhelming part by sifting through these practices and zeroing in on the few, or even the one, that will deepen your roots most in this season of your life and leadership. How does that sound?

Since the time of Saint Benedict, a term has been used to describe the blueprint for building our spiritual-root system: a "Rule of Life." Benedict himself wrote a small book to lay out the Rule of Life for his original community; his rule addressed the organizational-logistical side of their lives together as well as the spiritual-transformational side of their Godward activities. Benedict's rule has been a guide for countless Christ followers since, both monastics and others.

The term *rule* carries with it some negative connotations in our modern culture: It can easily sound harsh and rigid. And within the monastic tradition, sometimes it was. But once we hear the heartbeat of God in it—the stabilizing force of being the beloved, the abundance that leads us to conversion, and the security of surrendering in obedience—all harshness and rigidity falls away. In its place, we are left with a solid sense of self, an enduring intimacy with God, and an exhilarating partnership of vocation.

This is what it means to be a monk in the marketplace.

In the following pages, you will have the chance to articulate your own spiritual rhythms, the ones you sense God calling you to engage in during this season. By defining those and making space for them in your days, you will carve out a river bed for the "living water" to flow through your life. Without such a conduit, the living water gets dissipated like a swamp. *How much structure do you need?* Just enough to keep the life of God moving forward in a direction that is true to your soul and calling.

Becoming and Doing

Another treasure from the monastic heritage is the belief that our spiritual journeys consist of two complementary dynamics: *action* and *contemplation*. Neither of these channels is adequate without the other. We must become, and we must do. We must be transformed, and we get to partner with God in transforming. Simple. These two go together as naturally as peanut butter and chocolate. Except that I don't like peanut butter, so I'll say . . . like dark chocolate and a vintage port. Or bourbon and a cigar. You get the point.

You don't have to be a rocket scientist to notice that our culture is all about action and little about contemplation, which is why this book leans toward the contemplative side. Historically there have been times when the Christian community focused on contemplation at the expense of action; in those days, the prophetic voice had to say, "Stop being still and get busy." In this era, however, we have pushed the pendulum far, far out on the side of activity at the expense of stillness. By the grace of God, we must find a way to carry both forward as spiritual leaders, discerning what God is saying in this day and encouraging those around us to move in that direction.

The metaphor of the pendulum seems to invite us toward the idea of balance. Enough of this and enough of that to hold both. That's not a bad image, but recently I'm finding less inspiration from the idea of balance and more energy in the concept of *integration*. This moves me away from compartmentalization—trying to make sure I have exactly as many contemplative components as I have active components—and toward more cohesion in my life where the contemplative and the active are intertwined in a unity of being and doing. Perhaps it's all semantics, but this image is helping me these days.

Speaking of integration, let's take one last look at our emotional programs for happiness, again through the lens of Jesus and his inaugural temptations in the desert before being released into public ministry. As the prototype Christian, Jesus modeled the life we are called to lead, and his archetypal temptations mirror those we all face repeatedly.

First is the temptation to turn stone into bread—the urge to meet his legitimate need for *safety and security* in his own strength. Jesus counters with the truth that God alone is our security.

His second temptation is to dazzle the world by throwing himself off the Temple and floating safely down with an angelic escort. Such a display would have certainly won him the *approval and affection* of the masses. Jesus says no. When we know we have God's approval (remember his baptism?), then we don't have to put God to the test.

Finally, Jesus is tempted to win *power and control* over the entire world. All he has to do is betray his truest self and deepest convictions by worshiping what is false. But Jesus is already confident in God's rule and has surrendered himself fully to its claim on his life. Now it's our turn.

Let's Do This!

Now that we have explored our core principles and practices, it's time to build our own rhythms. There is no "right" way to go about this, but some ways are more conducive than others. I recommend getting out of your normal life space and into a fresh new space to complete this exercise. Take a personal retreat (chapter 9) for a weekend or even a single day and engage a discernment process (chapter 7). Discernment is really what's going on here. You are in dialogue with God about what you want of God and what God wants for you. It's not mysterious; really it's quite normal and accessible.

It is superhelpful to name the season you're currently in—not "the spring," but your season of life. Maybe you'll define your season by your current occupation or project: *I'm in the "norming" phase of my business launch;* or *I'm a working single mom of an adolescent;* or *I'm in a succession transition so I can retire.* Maybe you're a recent empty nester or you're trying to sell your business or launch a new product line. Or maybe you want to simply look at your season chronologically and take one calendar year at a time.

Questions

Here are some helpful questions to bring to God in your personal retreat space:

1. How would I describe my current life season?

2. My season of life contains these spiritual leadership opportunities and challenges:

3. I'd like to craft a Rhythm of Life for approximately this time period:

4. Which practices call most deeply to my heart, and why?

5. Which practice speaks to a particular need at this particular time?

6. Which practices fit my soul easily and naturally?

7. Which ones stretch or intimidate me? What is God saying to me about that?

Contemplative practices are often conceived as purely private, but that is a mistake. Many of them do indeed lend themselves to personal times of solitude, but almost all of them contain a communal dimension as well. You can do Centering Prayer with your spouse (if he or she is up for it). You can do discernment with your executive team. You can work through the Enneagram with your small group. Spiritual direction is obviously done with a mature spiritual guide. The Welcome Prayer can be done around your breakfast table. Wherever you experience spiritual community, you can practice together.

8. Which side of my spiritual journey needs more development right now—personal or communal?

9. What is one practice that is already life-giving that I might be able to replicate on the other side—either finding a

communal expression of a personal practice or a personal expression of a communal practice?

You are a leader in some capacity right now, whether it's in the boardroom, the family room, the church, or the community—or in all of these. For the sake of others in their sphere of influence, leaders naturally want to reproduce what's working for them. That could be one definition of leadership.

Here's the thing. No matter how jazzed you are right now about a new spiritual insight or practice, your words will carry more weight once that insight or practice has been seeded into your life and has begun to grow. The small group you are engaging as you go through this book is the best garden to experiment in as you wrestle with ideas and try new experiences on for size. You may not have to wait years, but wait until your gravitas seeds have sprouted and begun to bear a little fruit before you try to get everyone else planting too.

As you saw in this chapter's epigraph, Benedict conveyed the following timeless wisdom to his disciples: that leading by example is what gives gravitas to our leading with words. Both are important, but modeling comes first.

10. How can I use my leadership influence to invite others into the practices that are life-giving to me now?

Selecting from Your Color Palette

I have described fifteen specific spiritual practices in these chapters, each of them accessible for any reader. Obviously, this is not an exhaustive list, but it's a great start. A great palette, if you will, to draw color from as you paint the landscape of your life on the canvas of this season. Please do not try to implement them all at once; you don't get spiritual points for racking up the highest number. Again, this is a discernment exercise that is unique to you and to this moment in time.

Overview

As you scan back over the principles and practices we've covered in each chapter, listen for what the Holy Spirit is saying to your heart about each and write your responses to the questions below (or in a separate journal).

1: SPIRITUAL GRAVITAS

- What kind of weight or influence do you want for your leadership?

- How would you describe your life mission?

2: STABILITY

- What kind of relational, geographic, or internal stability is calling to you?

- How do you want to experience your belovedness in this season?

3: CONVERSION

- What awareness of your true self and false self is God inviting you into?

- How are you experiencing—or wanting to experience—God's abundant provision for you in this season?

4: OBEDIENCE

- What is God wanting to heal or realign in your life right now?

- How are you learning to surrender to the good purposes of God?

5: PRAYER

- How are you learning to pay attention to God, your soul, and your life?

- Of our three prayer practices (Welcome Prayer, Praying the Hours, Daily Examen), which are you feeling might be most impactful in your journey at this time?

6: STUDY

- In what ways are you feeling drawn toward wisdom, meditation, and self-study?

- Of our three study practices (Enneagram, Lectio Divina, spiritual direction), which are you feeling might be most important for you right now?

7: WORK

- What percentage of your current work experience falls within what you consider to be your vocation?

- Of our three work practices (discernment, culture crafting, group discernment), which are you most excited about?

8: HOSPITALITY

- How are you feeling drawn to welcome "the stranger" in your world?

- Of our three hospitality practices (Centering Prayer, giving, service), which one has your name on it immediately?

9: RENEWAL

- What specifically in your life needs renewal right now?

- Of our three renewal practices (Sabbath, personal retreats, sabbatical), which might be most impactful in your journey now?

Finding Your Rhythm

The final part of this exercise has to do with establishing daily, weekly, monthly, quarterly, and annual practices. In the last section, you named some practices you felt drawn to—or that felt important right now. By assigning those practices to recurring cycles and developing them as habits, these tools shift from wishes to plans.

Bear in mind that, as I like to tell my clients, it's all a big experiment. That takes the pressure off to "get it right" the first time. You have permission to play with these practices and see how they fit you. You can try them before you "buy" them. This is not a skill set to master or a performance to prove your worth; this is a safe place to grow into who you are meant to be in relationship with self, God, and the world. So where will you start? You can change at any time.

CONCLUSION

DAILY PRACTICES

-
-
-
-

WEEKLY PRACTICES

-
-
-
-

MONTHLY PRACTICES

-
-
-
-

QUARTERLY PRACTICES

-
-
-
-

ANNUAL PRACTICES

-
-
-
-

I mentioned that you can switch, edit, or update your practices at any time, and that's true. It's also wise to set a *recurring review* for your Rhythm of Life, perhaps quarterly or annually or whenever you feel like one season is coming to a close and another is beginning. A regular review of your practices can be one of your practices.

What Do You Want Most?

In Matthew 26:6-13, Jesus made a strange move when the disciples criticized Mary of Bethany for "wasting" expensive perfume on his feet. "This perfume could have been sold at a high price and the money given to the poor," they protested. Jesus' reply, "The poor you will always have with you," is unexpected given his ministry focus on the poor—until you realize he's not diminishing the plight of those in practical need; instead he's making a point that there are even higher priorities. And the same is true for us today: The practical responsibilities of our vocational lives are important, and they will always be there—ready, waiting, demanding. But our worship and transformation are even higher priorities, ones that release us from being ruled by tasks and give us the roots to be even better at our tasks.

What is remarkable about Mary is how she responded to her deepest desire. The yearning she felt to root herself in God was a force that drove her to defy social conventions—to break the stereotype of men-only disciples and sit as Jesus' feet (Luke 10:39), drinking in his every word. And here in the perfume scene, she makes the disciples highly uncomfortable with her effusive, intimate offering. But instead of redirecting Mary's attentions or merely tolerating them, Jesus elevates her courageous action in unprecedented fashion: "Truly I tell you, wherever this gospel is preached throughout the world, what she has done will also be told, in memory of her" (Matthew 26:13).

Personally, I haven't heard many sermons about this phenomenal act of worship, but this should be one of the great messages of all time. And the subtext of this story offers implicit questions: *How far are you willing to go to root yourself in the continual presence of God? Whose good opinion are you willing to give up? What protocols are you willing to break to have your heart's desire?*

Extending Your Branches

Your roots are already growing. Can you feel it? Now it's time to extend your branches of influence. How far should your influence go? That's up to God. But whatever your sphere, you now get to sow the seeds of your God-life in them. If you lead a work group, they are your "disciples." If you lead a company, they, too, are your disciples. Whether they are spiritually minded or not is irrelevant. Whether they are Christians or Buddhists or atheists doesn't matter as much as your opportunity to influence. You are there to serve and to demonstrate the Kingdom of God among them—never to force or impose; always to serve.

Start by building a coalition of those who are like-minded. Soak your workplace in prayer. Shepherd your leadership team by caring for their souls as well as their productivity. Look for ways to actively educate your workplace community and shape that culture in ways that line up with God's character. Look for ways to serve the poor and marginalized. Level the field of power. Model humility.

Never underestimate the power of a Godward life. Your values, your practice, and your ethics all have an impact. Your intent to use your influence to further God's interests in the world has an impact. Your efforts to craft a spiritually and emotionally healthy culture in your workplace all have an impact. Depending on your position in the marketplace arena, you can determine which values can be mandated, which can be encouraged, and which must simply be modeled. But take up the mantle you have been given. God is waiting to partner with you. Amazing, isn't it?

How will you know if you are carrying God's purposes in God's way? Easy: *It will start with love. It will end with love. And it will be marked by love throughout.* Whenever you run into angry Christians, you can be sure that they have gotten lured off the path of Christ (and we've all gotten entangled there at times). First Corinthians 13 reminds us that no matter how phenomenal our spiritual practice, if it's not rooted and grounded in love, it is worthless. Leadership with the attitude and character of Jesus will be saturated in love for our families, our spiritual communities, our work groups, our clients and customers, our cities, and our world.

The Endgame

God has an endgame for planet Earth, and it's the return of Christ. The physical return of Jesus will blow our minds and sweep us off our feet; I really cannot fathom it. But let's not wait for that. Let's *be* the return of Christ. Let Christ dwell richly in us and through us (Colossians 3:16)! The earth is waiting ("groaning," Paul says), yearning for God's children to be revealed (Romans 8:19-23), hungry for women and men of spiritual integrity to step up and step out in the marketplace with the authority of

Christ. Don't confuse this with political agendas; those are not God's primary interest (Matthew 22:21). God's interest is ruling in your domain through those who are rooted in contemplation and ready for action.

What will be the outcome of such rooted ruling? Nothing less than spiritual healing and reconciliation. Remember some of the last words Jesus uttered before he ascended:

> I pray also for those who will believe in me through their message, that all of them may be one, Father, just as you are in me and I am in you. May they also be in us so that the world may believe that you have sent me. I have given them the glory that you gave me, that they may be one as we are one . . . so that they may be brought to complete unity. Then the world will know that you sent me and have loved them even as you have loved me.
>
> JOHN 17:20-23

Jesus came to bind up the divisions and alienations of planet Earth, to reconcile people to God and to one another so they can enter the life of the Kingdom. That process begins in this world and continues in the next. This is not just a job for professional ministers; this is a calling for us all. The world needs you to lead with courage and strength.

With gravitas.

Epilogue

A Day in the Life of a Benedictine

IN SEPTEMBER of 2017, I spent four days at Belmont Abbey, a Benedictine community just west of Charlotte, North Carolina. Having only been in a Catholic service once before, I didn't really know what to expect. But I was warmly greeted by Brother Edward, who showed me the ropes and invited me into the monastic life, however briefly.

A surprisingly youthful-looking fifty-year-old, Brother Edward flashed a broad smile and a broad enthusiasm for his role as guest-master. Fastidious in manner, he toured me in and around the building and grounds, quick to offer an encouraging thumbs-up at every turn. The other brothers were more aloof, greeting me in the hall with a solemn nod but holding their space in silence.

The brothers started their day with vigils at 6:00 a.m., a beautiful awakening of the soul in melodic chanting of hymns and antiphonal Psalm readings, punctuated by solo readings and silent reflection. The high-pitched voices resonated softly within the 1893 basilica of Gothic splendor as they welcomed the day with quiet praise. Despite the foreignness of it, my soul was strangely stirred. And although I wasn't fully awake at this hour, I found myself grateful that the modern Benedictines had cut their daily prayer sessions from eight to four . . . and nudged vigils from midnight to 6:00 a.m.! Then we headed to breakfast, a simple affair of fruit, cereal, and bread taken in quiet.

Lauds came quickly at 7:30 a.m. for more of the same—cantor-led chanting, readings, and prayer. It lasted perhaps twenty minutes. I quickly got the impression that prayer is the anchor of the Benedictine identity and daily rhythms, even as the monastery itself is the anchor of their physical presence. This stands in contrast with other monastic orders such as the Jesuits, who take no stability vow and have more of a missional orientation, traveling frequently. But the prime passion and calling of the Benedictines is to prayer and their community. Because Belmont Abbey is attached to a college, they also have a strong presence among the students. As Edward walked me around campus, every soul who passed smiled and waved, a pleasure unexpected in the modern collegiate environment.

The morning provided four hours of uninterrupted time for me, time to read and write. The monks busied themselves with the practical affairs of the day—cleaning, preparing for services, running errands, working in the kitchen, offering spiritual direction to the community, and engaging in their own reading and studies. My room on the top floor was singularly quiet.

Midday prayer was signaled by an insistent ringing in the bell tower, eight minutes before the 11:45 a.m. start. The twenty-two monks filed quietly into the basilica, bowing toward the altar before taking their places in choir boxes facing one another across the chancel. Ages ranged from twenties to nineties. All wore the same black habit, a full robe covered by long folds of cloth in the front and back that reached to the floor, with a hood in the back and no rope, just a belt. After prayer, they filed out reverently but got chatty on the walk to lunch.

Lunch was both nutritious and delicious, creative combinations of vegetarian fare: a mix of rice, corn, and something green; roasted sweet potatoes and carrots; lentils and green beans; and a soup of curried tomatoes and zucchini.

In the afternoon, Brother Edward invited me to walk through the Grotto of Our Lady of Lourdes on our way to a small chapel made of soaring wooden beams and walls of leaded glass. The back wall was entirely transparent behind the large crucifix, offering a worshipful view of lush forest—my kind of place. A handful of students and adults bowed in prayer or read quietly in the intimate space. I had brought a book but found myself caught up in the holy quiet. I was reluctant to break the spell of the place when Edward touched me on the shoulder and signaled that it was time to leave.

I peppered him with questions: *When did God first become real to you? What made you decide to become a monk? What do you do all day? Can you drink alcohol? What's the difference between a cathedral and a basilica? Do you own anything?*

Mass came at 5:00 p.m., and I felt less connection with this more formal event. Although it contained some of the same prayer elements as before, the action centered around the elaborate preparation, presentation, and service of the Eucharist. Adorned with vestments rather than a habit, the abbot approached the massive marble altar to engage in the ceremonial washing, a complicated ritual that included the elements, ancient prayers, kneeling and bowing, and offering of wafer and wine (not to me, though, because I'm not Catholic). The brothers served one another, and the smattering of public faithful scattered across the vast chamber.

Before dinner, Brother Edward invited me to tour the abbey graveyard. The expansive grounds apparently served the larger community, but at the center lay great monuments to commemorate past abbots, beginning with Leo Haid, the founding abbot-bishop of Belmont, who was born in 1849 and died in 1924. Edward then directed me toward the back-left corner of the grounds that held neat rows of identical headstones marking the graves of all monks who had served and died there for the past 141 years.

"I knew the last seven of these," Edward said fondly, then offered a couple of sentences to describe each. "I'll be buried here too," he mentioned matter-of-factly. The weight of their vows of stability struck me with force; all twenty-two of these men would spend their entire lives almost completely defined by several acres right there in Belmont, North Carolina. They would wake up each morning to pray, eat, study, and serve quietly, year after year, until they died. Then they would get their own personal headstones in that very field. *Wow. Gravitas.*

During dinner (chicken pot pie, rice, and spinach), one of the monks read aloud from a biography on the life of Stanley Rother (a missionary priest martyred in Guatemala in 1981) while all the brothers listened and ate. Apparently this was their normal dinner tradition. It reminded me of the many books read in my family when I was a kid; this was their family.

The last prayer of the day was compline at 7:00 p.m. I was starting to get the hang of following the hauntingly beautiful melody lines. The gentle strength of those sacred words washed over me and pulled my soul down into the ground of my being. I liked it.

I'm not a monk. Not really. Sometimes I like to think of myself as a monk, but I have chosen neither poverty nor chastity nor obedience to an abbot. I have taken no vow of commitment to a single pin on a map. I will not be buried in that field, and many of the trappings of "high church" feel ostentatious to me. Still, I found myself wondering what this life would be like for more than a few days.

As I drove away from Belmont Abbey Sunday morning after lauds, I reflected on my brief time with these men. I wasn't ready to trade my blue jeans for a black robe. I was definitely not tempted to trade my wife for twenty-two roommates. But there was a richness there—a richness I believed I could weave into the fabric of my own life. A richness that I was already weaving, and that you can weave in, too, if you're so inclined. Start with the practices I've talked about in this book. And if you ever get the chance, sign up for your own little retreat at a monastery. You just might like it.

Resources

FOR A LARGE SELECTION of tools and resources for Christian leaders, go to my website at www.Thrive9Solutions.com/resources for free downloads. You will find the resources listed below, as well as others.

- Welcome Prayer Guide
- Praying the Hours Guide
- Daily Examen Guide
- Enneagram Guide
- Lectio Divina Guide
- Spiritual Direction Guide
- Discernment Guide
- Culture-Crafting Guide
- Group-Discernment Guide
- Centering Prayer Guide
- Sabbath Guide
- Personal Retreat Guide
- Sabbatical Guide

Acknowledgments

MOST BOOKS ARE WRITTEN by a single individual, yet no book is birthed outside of a community. This is my chance to thank a few of the people and groups who have contributed so richly to my journey in writing this book.

Without question, the greatest human investment in this volume—and the life behind it—comes from my wife, Kellie. In the many times I have doubted myself, she has believed in me and who I am becoming, often urging me toward the Divine Presence and sharing a continuous flow of insights from her own journey. Ours is an unusually delightful partnership, for which I am profoundly grateful.

I want to thank the retreat centers that provided the solitude, beauty, and spiritual space for my writing: St. Francis Springs Prayer Center in Stoneville, North Carolina; Well of Mercy in Hamptonville, North Carolina; the Episcopal hermitages in Valle Crucis, North Carolina; Belmont Abbey in Belmont, North Carolina; and Fairhaven Ministries in Roan Mountain, Tennessee. I am most appreciative for the contemplative and restorative vision that drives each of your facilities, staff, and leadership.

Two extended times in communal study have shaped the contours of my soul in huge ways: first with Father Tim Patterson in The Servant Leadership School in Greensboro, North Carolina, and later with Ruth

Haley Barton at the Transforming Center in Chicago, Illinois. The years spent in these communities have enlarged my understanding and experience of God in life-defining ways.

I am deeply grateful for a handful of soul companions who have walked with me in the trenches of life and participated in the formations represented in these pages: Jeff Malesovas, Mark Maltby, John Freeman, Anthony Shelton, and Lisa Harrell. I am wealthy in friendships. Thanks, too, to the late-night TC wine club: Jenna, Marilyn, Hope, Meg, Tom, Cliff, and Desiree. You guys rock.

My greatest thanksgiving and adoration go to the Lover of my soul, who keeps drawing me—with astounding kindness and gentle transformation—toward the True Life.

Notes

INTRODUCTION

1. Online Etymology Dictionary, s.v. "gravitas (n.)," accessed August 9, 2019, https://www.etymonline.com/word/gravitas.
2. Bertrand Russell, "In Praise of Idleness," *Harper's Magazine*, October 1932, https://harpers.org/archive/1932/10/in-praise-of-idleness/.
3. A scan of the original source, John Maynard Keynes, "Economic Possibilities for Our Grandchildren (1930)," is available here: http://www.econ.yale.edu/smith/econ116a/keynes1.pdf.
4. Lydia Saad, "The '40-Hour' Workweek Is Actually Longer—by Seven Hours," Gallup, August 29, 2014, https://news.gallup.com/poll/175286/hour-workweek-actually-longer-seven-hours.aspx.
5. Susan Shinn Turner, "Janet Ward Black Relies on 'God's Math' to Give Back to Community," *Salisbury Post*, November 28, 2018, https://www.salisburypost.com/2018/11/28/janet-ward-black-relies-on-gods-math-to-give-back-to-community/.
6. Contary to common belief, a tree's roots are not precise mirror images of its branches (hence my use of the word *roughly* here); Portland Parks & Recreation, "Tree Physiology Primer—All about Roots!," accessed August 21, 2019, https://www.portlandoregon.gov/parks/article/587789.

1: SPIRITUAL GRAVITAS

1. Henri Nouwen, *In the Name of Jesus* (New York: Crossroad, 1989).
2. Thomas Keating, *The Human Condition: Contemplation and Transformation* (Mahwah, NJ: Paulist Press, 1999), 13–18.

2: STABILITY

1. Anthony Marett-Crosby, ed., *The Benedictine Handbook* (Collegeville, MN: Liturgical Press, 2004), 81.

2. Carole King, "So Far Away," *Tapestry*, copyright © 1971 A&M Records.

3. M. Robert Mulholland Jr., *The Deeper Journey: The Spirituality of Discovering Your True Self* (Downers Grove, IL: IVP, 2006), 47.

4. Ruth Haley Barton, *Strengthening the Soul of Your Leadership: Seeking God in the Crucible of Ministry* (Downers Grove, IL: IVP Books, 2008), 19.

3: CONVERSION

1. Parker J. Palmer, *The Active Life: A Spirituality of Work, Creativity, and Caring* (New York: John Wiley & Sons, 1999), 124–25.

2. "The Rule of Saint Benedict," The Friends of St. Benedict, accessed July 29, 2019, http://www.benedictfriend.org/the-rule.html.

3. *"Every one of us is shadowed by an illusory person: a false self."* Thomas Merton, *New Seeds of Contemplation* (New York: New Directions, 2007), 34.

4. "Sarx," Bible Study Tools, accessed July 29, 2019, http://www.biblestudytools.com /lexicons/greek/nas/sarx.html.

5. Bobb Biehl, *Fourth Grade: The Single Most Shaping Year of a Person's Existence* (DVD lecture), https://bobbbiehl.com/product/fourth-grade/.

6. William A. Barry and Robert G. Doherty, *Contemplatives in Action: The Jesuit Way* (Mahwah, NJ: Paulist Press, 2002), 28.

7. Brené Brown, "Boundaries," interview by The Work of the People, accessed September 26, 2019, http://www.theworkofthepeople.com/boundaries.

8. Richard Rohr, "Scarcity or Abundance?" Center for Action and Contemplation, January 29, 2016, https://cac.org/scarcity-or-abundance-2016-01-29/.

9. C. S. Lewis, *The Weight of Glory and Other Addresses* (New York: HarperOne, 2001), 45–46.

4: OBEDIENCE

1. Wm. Paul Young, *Eve: A Novel* (New York: Howard Books, 2015).

2. Jim Collins, *Good to Great: Why Some Companies Make the Leap . . . and Others Don't* (New York: HarperBusiness, 2001), 21–25.

3. Patrick Lencioni, *The Ideal Team Player: How to Recognize and Cultivate the Three Essential Virtues—A Leadership Fable* (Hoboken, NJ: Jossey-Bass, 2016).

4. Rick Warren, *The Purpose Driven Life: What on Earth Am I Here For?*, expanded ed. (Grand Rapids, MI: Zondervan, 2012), 150.

5: PRAYER

1. "The Rule of Saint Benedict," The Friends of St. Benedict, accessed July 30, 2019, http://www.benedictfriend.org/the-rule.html.

2. *Cast Away*, directed by Robert Zemeckis, written by William Broyles Jr., featuring Tom Hanks (20th Century Fox and DreamWorks, 2000).

3. Plato, *Apology*.

4. St. Ignatius, "Rules for the Discernment of Spirits," in *The Spiritual Exercises of*

St. Ignatius of Loyola, trans. Elder Mullan (New York: P. J. Kenedy & Sons, 1914), 177–80, https://archive.org/details/TheSpiritualExercisesIgnatius/page/n199.

5. Patrick Barry et al., *Wisdom from the Monastery: The Rule of St. Benedict for Everyday Life* (Collegeville, MN: Liturgical Press, 2005), 10.
6. David G. Benner, *Desiring God's Will: Aligning Our Hearts with the Heart of God*, expanded ed. (Downers Grove, IL: IVP Books, 2015), 33.
7. The Liturgy of the Hours used Latin names meaning "praise" (*lauds*), "sunrise" (*prime*), "third"—as in the third hour after dawn (*terce*), "sixth" (*sext*), "ninth" (*none*), "sunset" (*vespers*), "completion" (*compline*), and "watch" (*vigils*).
8. Wilfrid Stinissen, *Into Your Hands, Father: Abandoning Ourselves to the God Who Loves Us* (San Francisco: Ignatius, 2011), 62–63.

6: STUDY

1. Integrative9 Enneagram Solutions, "Enneagram History and Origins," accessed August 20, 2019, https://www.integrative9.com/enneagram/history/.
2. Lynn Quirolo, "Pythagoras, Gurdjieff and the Enneagram," Enneagram Monthly, accessed August 20, 2019, http://www.enneagram-monthly.com/pythagoras -gurdjieff-and-the-enneagram.html.

7: WORK

1. Bible Hub, s.v. "3000. latreuó," accessed August 20, 2019, https://biblehub.com /greek/3000.htm; Austin Burkhart, "'Avodah': What It Means to Live a Seamless Life of Work, Worship, and Service," March 31, 2015, https://tifwe.org/avodah-a -life-of-work-worship-and-service/.
2. Jim Collins, *Good to Great: Why Some Companies Make the Leap . . . and Others Don't* (New York: HarperCollins, 2001), 90–119.
3. Van Morrison, "On Hyndford Street," *Hymns to the Silence*, copyright © Polydor, 1991.
4. As quoted in Ruth Haley Barton, *Pursuing God's Will Together: A Discernment Practice for Leadership Groups* (Downers Grove, IL: IVP Books, 2012), 127.
5. Barton, *Pursuing God's Will Together*, 169–222.

8: HOSPITALITY

1. Richard Rohr, "Taking Jesus Seriously," Center for Action and Contemplation, September 17, 2017, https://cac.org/taking-jesus-seriously-2017-09-17/.
2. See Luke 6:27-31 (nonviolence); Matthew 19:22-24 (dangers of wealth); Luke 4:17-19 (bias toward poor); Matthew 5:1-12 (Beatitudes).
3. Catherine de Hueck Doherty, *Poustinia: Christian Spirituality of the East for Western Man* (Combermere, ON: Madonna House, 1993).
4. World Heritage Encyclopedia, s.v. "Poustinia," accessed August 20, 2019, http:// www.gutenberg.us/articles/Poustinia.
5. "Madonna House—Ottawa, ON," Madonna House, accessed August 6, 2019, http://www.madonnahouse.org/locations/madonna-house-ottawa.

9: RENEWAL

1. Fil Anderson, *Running on Empty: Contemplative Spirituality for Overachievers* (Colorado Springs: WaterBrook, 2004).

2. Stephen R. Covey, *The 7 Habits of Highly Effective People: Powerful Lessons in Personal Change* (New York: Free Press, 2004), 288–89.

3. Jerome Daley, *Soul Space: Where God Breaks In* (Brentwood, TN: Integrity, 2003), 167.

4. Dorothy C. Bass, ed., *Practicing Our Faith: A Way of Life for a Searching People* (Minneapolis: Fortress, 2019), 86, 76.

5. Mark Buchanan, *The Rest of God: Restoring Your Soul by Restoring Sabbath* (Nashville: Thomas Nelson, 2006), 89, 93.

6. Graham Cooke, *The Nature of God: Upgrading Your Image of God and Who He Wants to Be for You* (Tonbridge, UK: Sovereign World Limited, 2003), 22.

7. William A. Barry and Robert G. Doherty, *Contemplatives in Action: The Jesuit Way* (Mahwah, NJ: Paulist Press, 2002), 20–21.

8. Jeffrey M. Jones, "In U.S., 40% Get Less Than Recommended Amount of Sleep," Gallup, December 19, 2013, http://news.gallup.com/poll/166553/less-recommended-amount-sleep.aspx.

About the Author

JEROME DALEY is the founding coach for Thrive 9 Solutions, a consulting firm for Christian leaders in business and ministry. Making their home in the mountains of North Carolina, he and his wife, Kellie, are the parents of three grown children. Jerome has degrees in both ministry and business and is the author of ten books. His great delights are taking spiritual retreats, drinking good wine, backpacking in the mountains, and playing with his grandson. For more about Jerome's work, visit www.Thrive9Solutions.com.

Other books by Jerome include the following:

- *Soul Space*
- *When God Waits*
- *Not Your Parents' Marriage* (coauthor Kellie Daley)
- *The New Rebellion Handbook*
- *The Book of Days*
- *Following Jesus into the Power* (with Jerry Daley)
- *Following Jesus out of the Brokenness* (with Jerry Daley)
- *Following Jesus into the Blessing* (with Jerry Daley)
- *A Year of Thriving*

THE NAVIGATORS® STORY

THANK YOU for picking up this NavPress book! I hope it has been a blessing to you.

NavPress is a ministry of The Navigators. The Navigators began in the 1930s, when a young California lumberyard worker named Dawson Trotman was impacted by basic discipleship principles and felt called to teach those principles to others. He saw this mission as an echo of 2 Timothy 2:2: "And the things you have heard me say in the presence of many witnesses entrust to reliable people who will also be qualified to teach others" (NIV).

In 1933, Trotman and his friends began discipling members of the US Navy. By the end of World War II, thousands of men on ships and bases around the world were learning the principles of spiritual multiplication by the intentional, person-to-person teaching of God's Word.

After World War II, The Navigators expanded its relational ministry to include college campuses; local churches; the Glen Eyrie Conference Center and Eagle Lake Camps in Colorado Springs, Colorado; and neighborhood and citywide initiatives across the country and around the world.

Today, with more than 2,600 US staff members—and local ministries in more than 100 countries—The Navigators continues the transformational process of making disciples who make more disciples, advancing the Kingdom of God in a world that desperately needs the hope and salvation of Jesus Christ and the encouragement to grow deeper in relationship with Him.

NAVPRESS was created in 1975 to advance the calling of The Navigators by bringing biblically rooted and culturally relevant products to people who want to know and love Christ more deeply. In January 2014, NavPress entered an alliance with Tyndale House Publishers to strengthen and better position our rich content for the future. Through *THE MESSAGE* Bible and other resources, NavPress seeks to bring positive spiritual movement to people's lives.

If you're interested in learning more or becoming involved with The Navigators, go to www.navigators.org. For more discipleship content from The Navigators and NavPress authors, visit www.thedisciplemaker.org. May God bless you in your walk with Him!

Sincerely,

DON PAPE
VP/PUBLISHER, NAVPRESS